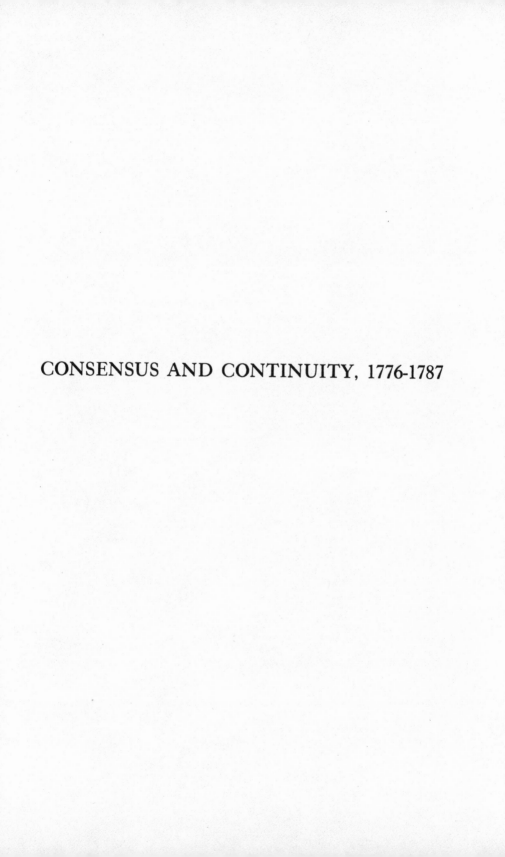

CONSENSUS AND CONTINUITY, 1776-1787

BOSTON UNIVERSITY • The Gaspar G. Bacon Lectures
on the Constitution of the United States

CONSENSUS AND CONTINUITY, 1776-1787

by

BENJAMIN FLETCHER WRIGHT

GREENWOOD PRESS, PUBLISHERS
WESTPORT, CONNECTICUT

Library of Congress Cataloging in Publication Data

Wright, Benjamin Fletcher, 1900-
    Consensus and continuity, 1776-1787.

    (The Gaspar G. Bacon lectures on the Constitution of
the United States / Boston University)
    Reprint. Originally published: Boston, Mass. :
Boston University Press, 1958.
    1. United States--Constitutional history. 2. United
States--Politics and government--1783-1789. I. Title.
II. Series: Gaspar G. Bacon lectures on the Constitution
of the United States.
JK116.W7 1984   973.3'1   84-19120
ISBN 0-313-22951-1 (lib. bdg.)

Reprinted in 1984 by Greenwood Press
A division of Congressional Information Service, Inc.
88 Post Road West, Westport, Connecticut 06881

Printed in the United States of America

10 9 8 7 6 5 4 3 2 1

THE BACON LECTURESHIP

The Gaspar G. Bacon Lectureship on the Constitution of the United States was established in 1927 by Mrs. Robert Bacon of New York in honor of her son, at that time Secretary of the Board of Trustees of Boston University. After several terms in the Massachusetts State Legislature and two years as lieutenant-governor, Gaspar G. Bacon retired from active politics and joined the faculty of Boston University in the department of Government in 1938. His teaching career was interrupted by four years of service in World War II, which he foresaw well in advance of his fellow countrymen. His experience in politics, his brilliant record as Lieutenant-Colonel in Military Government in the European theatre, followed by a year of travel in South America and a year teaching at the University of North Carolina, were varied experiences which he hoped to share with students on his return to Boston University in September 1947. He died suddenly on Christmas Day, 1947. By gift and bequest he augmented the fund established by his mother and thus made possible publication of the lectures which bear his name. He himself inaugurated the series in 1927. Since that time lectures have been given annually by some eminent scholar or jurist in fulfillment of the terms of the deed of gift which reads, "The purpose of the Lectureship is to stimulate a study of the Constitution of the United States, its antecedents, history and doctrines, together with the results and implications thereof."

The Bacon Lectures for the academic year of 1956-57 were delivered by Dr. Benjamin Fletcher Wright, President of Smith College. Well known as a national leader in higher education for women, political scientists and historians regard him as one of the keenest interpreters of American constitutional history of our time. His contributions to this field include *American Interpretations of Natural Law*, 1931 and *The Growth of American Constitutional Law*, 1942.

Dr. Wright's lectures at Boston University in April, 1957, under the general title "Consensus and Continuity," contain much new thinking on the constitution as a progressive document. He is in general disagreement with Charles Beard's thesis that the document was in fact an instrument of conservatism drafted by property holding reactionaries. Dr. Wright sheds new light on the Framers and their intentions.

The Gaspar G. Bacon Lectures Committee

WARREN O. AULT
ALBERT R. BEISE
ALBERT MORRIS
LASHLEY G. HARVEY, *Chairman*

TO

A. R. W.

TABLE OF CONTENTS

Chapters

CONSENSUS AND CONTINUITY — 1776 - 1787

I. THE SPIRIT OF '76 RECONSIDERED

American historical scholarship has not always avoided a parochial point of view. The isolationism long since abandoned by students of our diplomatic history remains in areas where it is equally inappropriate. This has been eminently true of otherwise excellent discussions of the American Revolution. Where such leaders of the Revolution as John Adams, Jefferson, Madison, and Wilson were keenly aware of its precedents and of the relation of our governmental experience to that of other nations, the historians who have written about that great age have rarely followed their example to the extent of comparing it with other revolutions, ancient and modern.

When such comparisons are made, the Revolution, its course of political events, and above all its constitutional results, appear so exceptional as to approach the unique. It proceeded with a rare economy of violence. Reprisals between civilian patriot and loyalist there were, but they were mild when compared with those of the French Revolution, the Russian Revolution, or the Spanish Civil War. Disputes, intrigues, factionalism, and recrimination among the leaders were not unknown. Yet by and large, the leaders of 1776 were also the leaders in 1787. None had gone to prison, or been hanged or beheaded for treason or alleged counter-revolutionary activity. The military chief became the first president of the Republic and retired at his own choice; the author of the Revolutionary Manifesto was its first Secretary of State; two of its chief agitators, though their glitter was somewhat dimmed, were still prominent political leaders in their respective states. Though it cannot be said that the American Revolution was conducted with absolute decorum, or that the losing side suffered no hardship, it can be said that it was conducted with moderation and a respect for lawful procedure not frequently encountered in the many revolutions about which we have authentic information.

Most of these revolutions exhibit a typical pattern or cycle. They begin with moderate aims pursued by moderate men; these are displaced by victory for the extremists; then terror and dictatorship; and, not infrequently, reaction and restoration of the old order. This was not the cycle of the American Revolution. By the time independence was agreed upon the men who led us into the Revolution had a fairly definite conception of their goals. Surprisingly, in view of the failure of leaders who initiated such movements in other countries, they were able to achieve them. The revolt and the process of constitution-making did not get out of control nor depart radically from their plans and their aims.

Consider, for example, how different was the history of events in the English Revolution or Civil War of the 17th Century. That bitter struggle began in a movement of moderates who sought the redress of grievances through constitutional change. Moderate aims and means lost out to genuine revolution, proceeding through regicide, the Commonwealth, military dictatorship, and Restoration. Within twenty years the cycle was complete.

The French Revolution similarly began with a demand for moderate reform and the constitutionalization of the monarchy. Its first cycle ended twenty-five years later with the restoration of the Bourbons. In between came regicide, the Terror, dictatorship, the man on horseback— Napoleon, foreign conquest and defeat. Even then there was no final settlement. France has had nine constitutions since 1789 (more according to some counts); the United States has had one. That one faced and survived a bloody conflict, but the fact that it emerged from the Civil War unchanged in its fundamental structure, is evidence of the consensus it reflected on all but one issue.

The circumstances which existed between the First and Second World Wars in Germany, Italy, and Spain, were not identical, but in each of these countries an attempt to establish a more democratic, constitutional system gave way to dictatorship.

The Russian Revolution, though distinctive in important ways, followed the familiar pattern. The attempt of the moderates under Kerensky to establish a constitutional republic lasted only seven months. Then followed the Bolshevik Revolution and the long period of communist dictatorship with its continuous and systematic use of terror and its perennial purge of alleged traitors. The story of the Chinese Revolution is similar to the Russian, though it required a generation instead of seven months to move from Sun Yat Sen to Chiang Kai-shek to Mao Tse-tung.

Some who read these cursory generalizations about revolutions will argue that the comparisons and contrasts are not well founded, since the American Revolution was not in the same sense a revolution, but rather a war for independence. I think that the answer to that observation is twofold.

In the first place, the American Revolution was more than a war for independence. As the late J. Franklin Jameson made clear in his classic little book, *The American Revolution Considered as a Social Movement*, the economic, social, and religious changes which took place during those years were numerous and substantial. Royal authority and privilege based on it ceased immediately, as did payment of quitrents to the Crown and to Proprietors. Royal restrictions on land settlement were no longer in effect. In some of the states many large Tory estates were confiscated and most of these were redistributed in smaller holdings. Where entailment and primogeniture existed in 1776, they were generally abolished before the end of the Revolution. Important steps were taken toward religious equality and the separation of church and state. The penal code was ameliorated in several of the states. Many of the old and powerful families, except in parts of the South, took the side of Great Britain and lost power. Their place was taken by new leaders drawn from younger men, from the common people, and from the middle classes.

As Jameson put it, "The relations of social classes to each other, the institution of slavery, the system of land holding, the course of business, the forms and spirit of the intellectual and religious life, all felt the transforming hand of revolution, all emerged from under it in shapes advanced many degrees nearer to those we know."[1]

Secondly, if we look at the American Revolution as being primarily a war for independence, and then compare its course with wars for independence in other countries in this hemisphere, we find that most of them did not proceed along the same lines or follow the same process as in the United States. There were too many such revolutions in the 19th century to make possible individual comparisons, but it seems substantially accurate to say that in most of the wars for independence in Latin America the course of the struggles was neither smooth nor uninterrupted by the emergence of a military dictator. In many of these countries there were abrupt breaks in continuity, reaction followed by internal revolution or civil war. In some there is still lacking that basic agreement on fundamentals, that consensus, which characterized the establishment of independent government in the United States.

---

[1] *The American Revolution Considered as a Social Movement*, p. 11.

If the course of events and constitutional decisions in the years 1776-1787 was exceptional, was it because the leaders of that era were supermen? I think that there is a less idolatrous and more enlightening explanation for the variation from the experience of so many other countries, and that the way to it begins with an analysis of the Spirit of '76.

The pictorial representation of the Spirit of '76 is ordinarily three battered but triumphant figures marching to the music of fife and drum. That symbolism is not too far fetched, since Washington's army at times was not so very much larger or so much better equipped, but it has no particular relation to constitutional ideas and institutions.

There is, with one possible exception, no book of systematic political and constitutional philosophy, or any collection of such books, in which we can find a reflection of the ideas of that time. The exception is John Adams' *Defense of the Constitutions of Government of the United States of America,* an interminable work of three volumes, the first appearing in 1786, in time to be of influence in the Federal Convention. This collection of quotations, paraphrases, and comments was a defense of the separation of powers principle as embodied in the state constitutions, particularly that of Massachusetts. The fragmentary literature of that age—letters, speeches, pamphlets—is interesting and sometimes significant. But there is very little which helps us to understand the decisions that were made once independence was agreed upon.[2] This is in contrast with the great mass of literature of the preceding twelve years when the rights of the colonies, and colonists, were being warmly, frequently learnedly, debated.

There is, however, one great pamphlet published at the very beginning of the year 1776, some mention of which cannot possibly be omitted, Tom Paine's *Common Sense,* even though it is only partially representative of the Spirit of '76.

In a moment of pique or of ignorance, Theodore Roosevelt wrote that "Tom Paine was a dirty, little atheist." Paine was neither dirty, little, nor an atheist. His stature was and is impressive and our debt to him is not slight, but we are not indebted to him for governmental forms

---

[2] A recent discussion of this literature is found in Clinton Rossiter's *Seedtime of the Republic,* ch. XIV. See also M. C. Tyler's *Literary History of the American Revolution,* vol. II.

or constitutional principles. His great contribution was to the attainment of independence.

On January 9, 1776 this newcomer to America (he arrived in the fall of 1774) published in Philadelphia one of the most influential, as well as one of the most emotional and eloquent, tracts for the times. The pamphlet came at exactly the right time to influence the trend of events in America. Fighting had been going on for more than eight months, yet there had been no decision to fight for independence. The official position continued to be the recognition of dominion status and the redress of grievances. Paine was completely impatient with what he saw as a weak and indecisive attitude, as he was impatient with, and did not understand, the pamphlets and other writings of the preceding two years in which some of the ablest men of the colonies had argued in favor of membership in what we know as a commonwealth of nations. To this recent immigrant, "a government of our own is our natural right." His pamphlet is a diatribe against English monarchy, and a plea for independence as a goal. He was ignorant of history, of law, and of philosophy, but he saw no need for them.

He was particularly free in his condemnation of "the so much boasted Constitution of England . . . [which] is imperfect, subject to convulsions, and incapable of producing what it seems to promise." A "natural proof of the folly of the hereditary right of kings is that nature disapproves it. Otherwise she would not so frequently turn it into ridicule, by giving mankind an ass for a lion."

The tone changes sharply, though the emotion is even more apparent, when he pleads the case for independence.

"The sun never shined on a cause of greater worth. . . . to talk of friendship with those in whom our reason forbids us to have faith, and our affections wounded thro' a thousand pores instruct us to detest, is madness and folly.

"O! ye that love mankind! Ye that dare oppose not only the tyranny but the tyrant, stand forth! Every spot of the old world is overrun with oppression. Freedom hath been hunted round the Globe. . . . O! receive the fugitive, and prepare in time an asylum for mankind."

Later in the year 1776, when the Revolutionary cause seemed particularly desperate, Paine began the publication of the series of pamphlets called *The American Crisis*. The first number of this famous series began with the immortal phrase, "These are the times that try men's souls. . . . Tyranny like hell is not easily conquered . . . the harder the conflict, the more glorious the triumph." On April 19, 1783, just eight years after the fighting at Lexington and Concord, the last of the *Crisis* papers was published. It began with this sentence: "The times that tried men's souls are over—and the greatest and completest revolution the world ever knew, gloriously and happily accomplished."

Clearly Paine is one of the great propagandists. He was also, as Carl Van Doren once wrote,

> "[T]hat almost incredible thing, a tribune of the people without self-interest. The most influential author of his day, he had but a modest pride of authorship. He could have made his fortune a dozen times, but he lived and died in poverty—died the same Ragged Philosopher he had lived, under the full weight of ingratitude from the kingdom he had helped liberalize and the two republics he had helped establish."[3]

It is tempting to deal at greater length with Paine, but the fact of the matter is that his influence in America was limited almost entirely to accelerating the decision to fight for independence and to the effective propaganda which came from his pen during the course of the war. For Paine was a congenital, confirmed reformer, a sentimental optimist with an uncritical and an unbounded faith in the common man. He believed that if certain social, economic, and political evils were removed, man would be good and wise, and would behave that way. His hatred of kings and of the British social system, under which he had lived and been a failure before he came to the colonies, was congenial to most Americans, but beyond that point his views were not widely shared. He had no respect for lawyers, no understanding of the validity or significance of constitutional restraints on legislatures elected by vote of the people, no patience or comprehension of such a concept as freedom slowly broadening down. Paine wanted quick, radical, sweeping reforms—political, economic, social, and religious. He seemed never to fear what Jefferson called an "elective despotism," and he did not con-

---

[3] Introduction to the Modern Library edition of Paine's *Writings*. Van Doren's essay is warmly sympathetic, but uncritical. For a careful analysis of Paine's relation to American thought and action see Cecelia M. Kenyon, "Where Paine Went Wrong," *American Political Science Review*, XLV, no. 4, Dec. 1951, pp. 1086-1099.

sider the cost, or the danger of reaction, when reforms are instituted by decree backed up by force. In almost all of these views and feelings he was atypical of the American climate of opinion in the years 1776 to 1787.

Late in the winter or early in the spring of 1776 a number of the colonial legislatures asked the Congress, sitting in Philadelphia, the nature of what we should call the war aims. In effect they said, are we, or are we not, fighting for independence? On May 15, 1776, following long debate, the Congress voted what is clearly a decision to fight for independence. On July 2 the Congress adopted the resolution introduced on June 7 by Richard Henry Lee of Virginia, "That these United Colonies are, and of right ought to be, free and independent states. . . ." That is our real declaration of independence. Then on July 4th came the document whose official title is "The Unanimous Declaration of the 13 United States of America." We call it the Declaration of Independence, but independence had already been voted. This was a declaration stating the reasons and the justification for the vote in favor of independence as an objective. The nature of this historic document is made perfectly clear in the opening sentence, which concludes with the words, "a decent respect to the opinions of mankind required that they should declare the causes which impel them to the separation."

The importance of the Declaration is, of course, not limited to local circumstances of this particular controversy. It has, for 181 years, been one of the great statements of the principles of human freedom, largely because of the succinct eloquence with which Jefferson set forth the principles of free society in the opening sentences of his second paragraph:

"We hold these truths to be self-evident, that all men are created equal, that they are endowed by their Creator with certain unalienable Rights, that among these are Life, Liberty and the pursuit of Happiness. That to secure these rights, Governments are instituted among Men, deriving their just powers from the consent of the governed. That whenever any Form of Government becomes destructive of these ends, it is the Right of the People to alter or to abolish it, and to institute new Government, laying its foundation on such principles and organizing its powers in such form as to them shall seem most likely to effect their safety and Happiness."

The statement that the rights derived from nature include "Life,

Liberty and the pursuit of Happiness" is not notable for its niggardliness. The security of these rights is the justification for the existence of government. Moreover, only that government is just which derives its powers from the express consent of the governed. He was not a follower of Hobbes.

Though the Declaration of Independence is one of the great documents of history, a concise and masterly statement of the doctrines of consent and the right of revolution, it is possible to give it too comprehensive an application. Certainly Jefferson did not see it as more than an initial statement of war aims and the defense of independence. During the late spring of 1776, after the Virginia Assembly had taken the decision to adopt a constitution, he asked to be released from his duties as delegate to the Continental Congress, in order to return to Virginia and share in the framing of that constitution. Not justification of rebellion merely, but the construction of a new frame of government and a revised code of laws which would embody and make operative the principles of the Declaration was Jefferson's notion of the complete revolutionary. In this he was thoroughly representative of his times. Three states had adopted new constitutions even before the Declaration of Independence was voted (those of New Hampshire and South Carolina were intended as temporary in character and were soon replaced), and before the end of 1776, seven others did likewise, Connecticut and Rhode Island merely modifying their colonial charters to the new circumstances of independence. New York and Georgia followed suit in 1777, and Massachusetts in 1780. Thus before Yorktown, and while the outcome of the war was still in doubt, all thirteen states, and even the as yet unrecognized frontier community of Vermont, had either adopted new constitutions, or, as in the case of Rhode Island and Connecticut, adapted old charters to accord with the conditions of independence.

This great feat of constitution-making was unprecedented and remains unparalleled in the history of modern constitutionalism. The period of the Revolution was not, as the late Charles E. Merriam once wrote, "largely one of destruction."[4] It was one of creativity. In 1776 alone, eight new constitutions were written and adopted, and two old ones were modified. That year must therefore rank with 1787 as one of the two most significant years in the history of modern consti-

---

[4] *History of American Political Theories,* p. 98.

tution-making. Indeed it is likely that the latter year would have been one of failure rather than success, had it not been for the example, experience, and the constructive achievements of 1776 and the years immediately thereafter.

It is immensely significant of the Spirit of '76 and of the nature of American political thinking and action that these tiny and infant states should think it both natural and essential to have written constitutions as the basis for their governments, even when they were in a state of war. Rarely, if ever, did they debate the desirability of having a constitution. Rather they assumed that such documents were necessities. Their assumption can be understood only in terms of the long previous history of written constitutional documents in the colonies, and, in a somewhat different, but no less important sense in England.[5] Beyond this background of history and experience, is the fact, which I pointed out some years ago, "that all of the literature of protest" in the years between 1761 and 1776 "has as its basic principle the conception of government under law."[6] It was therefore only natural to the men of this time that, as John Adams tells us, as early as 1775 men's thoughts began to turn to the problem of establishing the legal basis for new governments in place of those which were at least temporarily in abeyance.[7] To the Americans it was not enough that there be revolutionary congresses or assemblies, though presumably representative of the patriotic citizens of the colonies. These representative bodies must govern in accordance with a known, settled, standing law. And from the first, and very temporary, constitutional document adopted by the Revolutionary Congress meeting at Exeter, New Hampshire in January, 1776 to the Constitution of Massachusetts, finally ratified and adopted in 1780, the evidence is clear and abundant that there was absolute consensus to the effect that a written constitution is a first essential of a free government.

Though all of the new states assumed the necessity of a written constitution as a basis for government, few of them immediately adopted

---

[5] B. F. Wright, "The Early History of Written Constitutions in America," *Essays in History and Political Theory* (1936), pp. 344-371.

[6] Wright, *op. cit.,* p. 360.

[7] John Adams, letter to Richard Henry Lee, Nov. 15, 1775, in *Works,* vol. IV, p. 185. See also his "Thoughts on Government," (January, 1776), *Works,* IV, pp. 193-195.

a special method for drafting and ratifying those constitutions. The distinction between fundamental law and merely legislative or statutory law was perfectly clear. Indeed, such a distinction had been central to the case against Parliament for more than a decade, just as it had been deeply rooted in colonial thought and experience for more than a century. Nevertheless, the origin or source of fundamental law was not so clear. Colonial charters had been either royal or proprietary in origin. The British Constitution was a conglomerate of royal charter, Acts of Parliament, judicial decisions, custom, and tradition. Its reality or essence as a constitution lay ultimately in the minds of men, in community consensus rather than in the precise origin of its ingredients. It was—and is—a true case of "thinking makes it so." A similar attitude seemed to be held by the authors of the earlier state constitutions, for the first of these were drafted and adopted by Revolutionary assemblies and were distinguished from ordinary legislation only by designation. Thus the Virginia Constitution, really the first of all American state constitutions, was the work of a convention composed of forty-five members of the House of Burgesses which assembled in Williamsburg on May 6, 1776. This convention was not elected by the voters for the purpose of drafting a constitution, and the constitution was not submitted to the people for approval or rejection. Some of the states did make use of specially elected conventions, but none of the constitutions of 1776 and 1777 was ratified by the people.

The first state to submit a constitution to the voters was Massachusetts. There the first proposal met with an overwhelming negative vote in 1778, partly because the document had not been prepared by a specially elected convention, partly because of inadequate separation of powers and checks and balances. The second, drafted for the convention of 1779 by John Adams, was accepted by a popular vote of at least 2 to 1, and then formally adopted by the reassembled convention. The process of drafting and adoption is the one later to be generally accepted throughout the Union.

Just as the new states groped their way toward a distinctive method of establishing fundamental law, so too did they proceed, unevenly and with several false steps, toward a method of changing a fundamental law once adopted. The history of the evolution of the concept of constitutional amendment, and of amending procedures, is exceedingly interesting.

The first constitutions adopted with the intention and expectation that they would be permanent, those of Virginia and New Jersey, did not contain amending clauses. No provision was made for changes that might be thought necessary or desirable in the future. At least, no regular procedure was prescribed for such changes. The Virginia Declaration of Rights did recognize the right of revolution, but this of course is a very different thing from a known and accepted method for effecting peaceful and limited changes in the constitution and therefore in the government.

The first state to include an amending clause in its new constitution was Delaware. The final article of its constitution, adopted September 21, 1776, contains the statement that certain parts of the constitution may not be changed "on any pretense whatever," but that other provisions in the constitution may be amended by a five-sevenths vote of the assembly. This extraordinary provision is an interesting and a curious combination of the constitutional theories of Oliver Cromwell and of William Penn. Certain provisions in the constitution are too fundamental ever to be altered, others may be changed only by a special majority. The latter idea, which is surely one of the most important inventions in the history of government, is directly descended from William Penn's Frame of Government for Pennsylvania of 1682, and from the Frame of Government for Pennsylvania and Delaware of 1683. Penn had prescribed six-sevenths as the majority necessary to amend; the Revolutionary constitution of Delaware reduced this to five-sevenths. So far as I have been able to determine, this is not only the first amending clause in a state constitution, but the first amending clause in any constitution other than the colonial frames of government written by Penn.

The Pennsylvania Constitution of 1776 contains a much more curious and, in practice, an unworkable provision for amendment through a convention called for this purpose by the Council of Censors, to be elected every seven years. Those who drafted this constitution made a definite division between fundamental and statutory law. They were also, it is evident, fond of strange and ingenious, though unworkable, devices.

The Maryland Constitution of November 11, 1776 allows amendment if the measure, after being passed by one legislature, is passed again by another newly elected. The Georgia Constitution of 1777 carries the principle of popular action further by requiring a petition for a convention which alone could adopt an amendment to be signed by a majority of voters in a majority of the counties. The Massachusetts Constitution of 1780, which had the most mature method of adoption, failed to achieve a similarly mature amending clause. It permits a convention to consider amendments if the General Court of 1795, upon the advice of the voters in the towns, shall so decide. No provision was made for amendments prior to that date, or afterwards.

None of these procedures for amendment proved entirely satisfactory, and all were subsequently changed. Yet taken together, they represent a significant advance in political theory and practice. A written constitution together with an amending clause was a means of securing continuity and change, stability and flexibility.

Just as the procedures for framing, adopting, and amending a constitution showed some confusion and variation with respect to carrying out fundamental principles upon which there was almost universal agreement, so too, did the constitutions themselves. They were all, except for that of Massachusetts, written hastily, at least by modern standards, sometimes by men urgently involved in the conduct of war. Their authors were not doctrinaire revolutionaries, with blueprints in their pockets for the world of the future. Nevertheless, they had clear ideas about what constituted good government. The new constitutions embody their principles, but they reflect, too, a certain amount of uncertainty or tentativeness in the application of these principles. This is particularly true of the separation of powers in theory and in practice. It is also evident in the bill of rights, which most of the constitutions contained. It is essential to an understanding of the basic assumptions and beliefs of that age to recognize that the bills of rights were parts of the fundamental law which limited legislative and executive powers, even though those offices of government were selected, directly or indirectly, by the people. They placed limitations upon the power of majority rule. The subsequent history of bills of rights and their interpretation in the United States supports this view, since the later removal of restrictions upon the suffrage led to or was accompanied by extension of these limitations on legislatures, as well as to general support for judicial enforcement of bills of rights. The argument of Alexander Hamilton in the 84th number of the *Federalist*—that a bill of rights is needed only as against a king—indicates, almost as clearly as his famous speech in the Federal Convention on June 18, 1787, that his political philosophy was in important respects as alien from that of the general body of American sentiment as were many of the views of his democratic antithesis, Tom Paine.

It is important to notice that the bills of rights are the work of men influenced both by English legal and constitutional traditions and by the philosophical writings of Locke, Sydney, and Milton. It is also evident that in them there is almost no evidence of the humanitarian sentiments, the "soft" attitudes toward women, children, and dumb beasts, found in the Massachusetts Body of Liberties of 1641, a document which among other things, made it a crime to practice law for profit. The Revolutionary bills of rights are libertarian rather than humanitarian.

The content of the rights whose protection is guarded in these bills of rights, or constitutional provisions partaking of their character, is variously stated, though there is a surprisingly small range of disagreement among the states. The most ambitious statement of all is the one in the opening paragraph of the Virginia Declaration of Rights: "The enjoyment of life and liberty, with the means of acquiring and possessing property, and pursuing and obtaining happiness and safety." Jefferson, writing a few days later, was content to refer to the pursuit of happiness. George Mason, the wealthy planter who drafted the Virginia Declaration of Rights, thought that men had a right not only to pursue but also to capture happiness and safety.[8]

Nearly all of the constitutions contained some statement about equality. The Virginia Constitution affirms that all men are by nature "equally free and independent." The Massachusetts provision (Article I of its Bill of Rights) asserts that "all men are born free and equal." It may here be observed that in no bill of rights, unless we include the frontier community of Vermont, which did not officially become a state until 1791, is the equality provision accompanied by the abolition of

---

[8] An interesting, and probably a fairly representative, view is expressed in a letter to the *Massachusetts Spy* written by a citizen of Hampshire County and published early in 1775: "Personal liberty, personal security and private property are the only motives, the grand objects for which individuals make a partial surrender of that plentitude of power which they possess in a state of nature and submit to the necessary restrictions, and subordinations of governments." Reprinted in the Pennsylvania Ledger, March 4, 1775. I owe this reference to Rossiter, *Seedtime of the Republic*, p. 410.

slavery. It seems evident that to most of the men of the Revolutionary era a declaration of equality did not run that far, any more than it included the principle that women should have equal legal rights with men or should share in the voting power. But in at least one state, Massachusetts, the Supreme Judicial Court held in 1783 that the provision concerning the equality of men had the legal effect of abolishing slavery, and slavery ceased to exist in that state from that day.

It is far from clear just what most of the men of '76 meant by equality, whether in the state bills of rights, or in the Declaration of Independence. Evidently they meant that Americans had equal rights with Englishmen. Most of them had a more ambitious, if rather vague, conception in mind: equality before the law, at least for free men; equality, that is, of legal rights, or equality in the power of asserting legal rights. It seems just as clear that few, if any, of the constitution makers had as simple a theory of equality as had Tom Paine, or one which was as sweeping and as inclusive.

Professor Elisha P. Douglass has argued, in his *Rebels and Democrats* (1955) that there were more egalitarians, in a sense which would have made them sharers in the point of view of Tom Paine, than has generally been recognized, though he of course concedes that these true democrats lost out except in Pennsylvania, and there the victory was not decisive nor enduring. To Professor Douglass the American Revolution would have been truly democratic if victory in the several states had resulted in the acceptance of simple majority rule, unicameralism, and complete equality of rights. In spite of his research and his cogent reasoning, there is little evidence that more than a few small groups of individuals favored anything approximating either economic equality or simple majority rule. Simple majority rule would not allow for the restraints on legislative action which became an increasingly important part of the American scene as an increasing proportion of adults came to have the vote. Nor is there reliable evidence that any large proportion of the population, or at least of that part which was articulate, favored a greater amount of social equality than that which was established during the Revolution.

For most men of that era equality did not have a nineteenth or twentieth century meaning. It is, for example, to be remembered that at the beginning of the Revolution there was a property qualification for voting in each of the colonies. At the end of the Revolution the property qualification remained except in four states where, for some or all offices, the payment of a public tax conferred the right of suffrage. In others the value of the property required had been reduced. A start had been made toward what was to become general, though not quite universal, in the first third of the nineteenth century, free adult male suffrage.[9]

The consent of the governed is a conception and a principle which is as evident in most of these constitutions as it is in the Declaration of Independence. It is clear enough, however, from the fact that property or tax qualifications for voting are to be found in all of them, that the conception was ordinarily interpreted to mean the consent of those who have some property, and that may be the principal, though it is not necessarily the only, meaning to be given to the Virginia phrase "having sufficient evidence of permanent common interest with, and attachment to, the community." Women, children, and slaves would have no institutional means of expressing their consent.

The consent of the governed applies not only to the carrying on of public business from day to day and year to year, it applies most explicitly to the establishment of a constitution. Indeed, it applies to the establishment of society itself, and it is clear that many of the constitution makers of this time thought of themselves as taking part in the formation of a social compact. The usual criticism of the social compact theory, that it lacks historical authenticity, does not apply in America. The Mayflower Compact and the early plantation covenants were examples of this principle in action, and the state constitutions of the Revolution are, if anything, even more perfect illustrations of social compacts, since the people in the colonies reverted to a state of nature, to use the language popular in the eighteenth century, when they separated from England. They then established by agreement new political systems. The preamble of the Massachusetts Constitution of 1780 is worth quoting on this point: "The body politic is formed by a voluntary association of individuals: It is a social compact by which the whole people covenants with each citizen and each citizen with the whole people that all shall be governed by certain laws for

---

[9] Professor Robert E. Brown, who has made a recent and careful study of voting in Massachusetts, concludes that the property qualification disenfranchised only a very small proportion of free adult males. *Middle Class Democracy and the Revolution in Massachusetts*, 1691-1780.

the common good." A clearer and more emphatic statement of the social compact theory is probably not to be found elsewhere in equally condensed form.

Guarantees of civil liberties are to be found in all of the Revolutionary bills of rights, and also in those constitutions of that period which contain no separate bill or declaration of rights. These guarantees are, for the most part, in the direct line of succession from the bills and petitions of rights which form so notable a part of English history in the seventeenth century, many of which trace their ancestry to Magna Charta.[10] The phrase translated from Magna Charta, "the law of the land", is more commonly found than the one which later becomes generally adopted in American constitutions, due process of law. The guarantees vary somewhat, but they generally include the rights of habeas corpus, of trial by jury in certain circumstances, usually a jury of the neighborhood or vicinity, of bail, of a free trial in open court. Frequently freedom of the press is included, in some freedom of religion also appears. The right to assemble and petition or remonstrate is found in most of the longer bills of rights; this is both an inheritance from England and a right which the colonial leaders had very recently employed—or been denied. The right of suffrage for all is not included among the natural or legal rights of men guaranteed in the bills of rights. But it is also to be noticed that the tendency toward liberalizing the qualifications for voting were such that only one state, South Carolina, had a religious qualification for voting by the end of this period. Only the Delaware Constitution prohibits the slave trade.

One of the somewhat surprising provisions encountered in these early bills of rights is what amounts to the right of revolution, even as against the government established under the Constitution, when the government fails to provide that freedom and security for which it was established. Thus the Virginia Constitution, after specifying the objectives of government, stipulates that "when any government shall be found inadequate or contrary to these purposes, a majority of the community hath an indubitable, unalienable and indefeasible right to reform, alter or abolish it, in such manner as shall be judged most conducive to the public weal."

---

[10] Z. Chafee, Jr., *How Human Rights Got into the Constitution* (1952).

If one reads that statement out of context, it can easily be taken as a doctrine of simple majority rule, as though Tom Paine rather than George Mason were the author of the Virginia Constitution. Such an interpretation is erroneous, partly because the spirit of the Virginia Constitution includes most explicitly the protection of minority rights, partly because of the suffrage limitations, partly because this constitution like all except one or two of those of the Revolution, provides for a system of separation of governmental powers. Indeed, it provides in two places for a separation of powers. The Declaration of Rights stipulates "that the legislative and executive powers of the state should be separate and distinct from the judiciary." The body of the Constitution provides that "the legislative, executive, and judiciary departments shall be separate and distinct, so that neither exercise the powers properly belonging to the other." This is almost as extreme a statement of the separation of powers as that written by John Adams, supported by an overwhelming vote of the citizens of Massachusetts in the town meetings, and ratified into the constitution of 1780. The final article in the Massachusetts Bill of Rights reads:

"In the government of this commonwealth, the legislative department shall never exercise the executive and judicial powers, or either of them: The executive shall never exercise the legislative and judicial powers, or either of them: The judicial shall never exercise the legislative and executive powers, or either of them: to the end it may be a government of laws, and not of men."

It is surely one of the most striking facts in the institutional and philosophical history of the United States that the legislative-executive quarrels during the colonial period convinced the colonists of the desirability of a separation of powers rather than a union of powers.[11] They had experienced more of separation and of checks and balances than was consistent with even moderately satisfactory government. Of course, they quickly abandoned the worst feature of the colonial system—the admixture of local and external control—but they continued to desire as much of separation as was compatible with the selection of the executive within the colony. It took just one year of constitution making in the states to develop the principle that the governor should be elected by the voters. In the first state constitutions the

---

[11] B. F. Wright, "The Origins of the Separation of Powers in America," *Economica* (London) May, 1933, pp. 176-179.

executive (in all of them except Pennsylvania a single executive) was elected by the legislative body or by one house of the legislature. But in 1777 New York adopted the constitution drafted originally by John Jay, later Chief Justice of the United States, which provided for a governor elected by popular vote. The example of New York was followed by Massachusetts in 1780, by New Hampshire in 1784 and, sooner or later, by all other states.

Some historians have seemed to find that the separation of powers was not the true expression of the point of view of the Revolution, primarily, if I understand their arguments, because the first group of constitutions had a less effective separation between executive and legislative bodies than the later ones, and in several of the early constitutions the upper house of the legislature was elected by the lower, as were the judges of higher state courts in some states. It seems to me that, considering the history of colonial governments and the controversies between governors and councils appointed by the Crown or by the proprietors and the elected lower houses, they provided for an astonishing amount of separation and of checks and balances in the very first constitutions. In the next group of constitutions, Georgia's alone excepted, there was a more effective separation of powers. The constitutions of Massachusetts and New Hampshire, adopted in 1780 and 1784, both of which were drafted by bodies elected especially for the purpose and both ratified only after popular vote in town meetings, contained the greatest separation of powers and checks and balances of any of the documents of the time.

In various ways, then, all of these constitutions give evidence of a sceptical view of human nature, of a distrust of popularly elected legislative and executive agents; none comes near to vesting as much unrestricted authority in government as does the French Declaration of the Rights of Man and of the Citizen, written in 1789. There one finds, after two articles which are reminiscent of the American bills of rights, the statement (Article III) that all sovereignty is in the nation, and a subsequent statement (Article VI) that "law is an expression of the general will." This is, from the point of view of the American principles accepted during the Revolution, much nearer to being totalitarian than to being pluralistic. The only limitation upon the expression of power seems to be the will of the nation, which is to say, the law of the national legislative body. The only effective restriction, other than the power of the suffrage would seem to be revolution. To the Americans of '76, '77 and '80 such doctrine was dangerous to liberty and the rule of law.

There is one other provision found in nearly all of the bills of rights of the Revolutionary era, one which I have intentionally left to the end, the right of property. Article one of the Virginia Declaration of Rights provides that the rights of citizens include "the means of acquiring and possessing property." Article one of the Massachusetts Bill of Rights, immediately after reference to life and liberty, guarantees the right "of acquiring, possessing, and protecting property." The three together add up to—"In fine, that [right] of seeking and obtaining their happiness and safety." To these authors of our first bills of rights, who were also leaders of the American Revolution, there was no thought of a conflict between civil rights on the one hand and property rights on the other. The right to acquire, possess, and be protected in the possession of, property was one of the most important of all civil rights. The conception of a conflict between civil and property rights is a development of the nineteenth century.

The thesis of this lecture has been that the political ideas of the American Revolution, the Spirit of '76, is not accurately represented by Tom Paine nor adequately by the Declaration of Independence. For that spirit is also to be found in the state constitutions of 1776, of 1777 and of 1780, constitutions which were, in many instances, written by the men who wrote and signed the Declaration of Independence.

To the men of this time there was no contradiction between the libertarian ideals of the Declaration of Independence and the limitations or restrictions of the state constitution. Contrary to what Charles Merriam and others have said, the age was immensely constructive, not merely destructive. The constitutions were essential to the attainment and protection of the rights asserted in the Declaration of Independence and also of those asserted in the state bills of rights. The leaders of '76 wanted protection and security for their liberties, and, to their way of thinking, protection was unattainable without a written constitution. They wanted order and stability as well as liberty, and to most of them order meant legal order. To them the ancient dilemma, liberty *or* stability, individual rights *or* authority was easily solved, for it was no dilemma at all. They believed that true authority was based upon liberty, and liberty required constitutional order.

These state constitutions were the most advanced, by far the most democratic, constitutions in the world at that time, but they were not documents of the kind which would have been acceptable to Tom Paine, or at least none except the atypical, and short lived constitution of Pennsylvania. That constitution provided, except for the strange mechanism of a Council of Censors, more reminiscent of Plato's *Laws* than of anything in the American experience, a relatively simple and almost majoritarian system. But even the Pennsylvania Constitution of 1776, one which was unpopular in that state almost from the first month of its establishment, contained constitutional restrictions upon the power of the legislative body and guarantees of individual rights.

The extent to which the various men and colonies demonstrated a consensus on political and constitutional principles is amazing, unless one realizes that they were drawing upon the reservoir supplied partly by the central stream of English development from Magna Charta to the Bill of Rights, but even more by the experience of self-government in the colonies. One can find some points of difference, even a few relatively peculiar features among the documents, including the constitutions, but the differences are slight indeed when one compares these constitutions with the forms and accepted principles of government in Europe, even in the mother country, England. The lasting effects of this consensus and of these decisions will be further considered in the next two chapters.

II. THE DIMENSIONS OF AGREEMENT AND THE RANGE OF COMPROMISE IN 1787

In the first chapter the American Revolution was contrasted with other revolutions of the last three centuries. Let me here pose a question similar to those comparisons and decidedly relevant to the interpretation of American history. Why has the American Constitution of 1787, as judged by the extremely important criteria of durability and adaptability, been the most successful written constitution of modern times?

Doubtless there are several answers to this question, but surely an essential one is that many of the most difficult decisions confronting any constitutional convention had, in effect though not by any specific action, been made before the Federal Convention met, even before its meeting was provided for.

Many years later, John Adams, in a letter to Jefferson, observed that the real revolution in America took place in the minds of the people, and that it took place before the fighting at Lexington and Concord. The people were ready for independence even though they had not begun to discuss it openly. Much the same can, I think, be said of the principal decisions made by the Convention of 1787.

While the Articles of Confederation was a remarkable document when the time and circumstances of its preparation are considered, it gives evidence both of inexperience with federal government and of distrust of any centralized power. In the few years of its existence it was found to be sadly inadequate to the needs of the country. The states remained virtually sovereign and, what was worse, many of them acted irresponsibly where national obligations were involved. Congress could not impose taxes but had to depend upon the states for contributions; its requests met with scant response and federal finances were soon in hopeless condition. It lacked both authority and money with which to defend the frontiers. Frequently there was no quorum in Congress to deal with the limited amount of business which could be carried on, and the machinery of government was as cumbersome as it was ineffective.

Perhaps the decisive weakness in the Articles lay in the amending clause. The Articles could be amended only by unanimous consent of the thirteen states. No amendment was ever adopted, since at least one state always refused to agree. If the Articles had been amendable, if, for example, that constitution could have been amended by three-fourths of the states rather than all of the states, it might have been adapted to the needs of the country; it might be the constitution of the United States in the twentieth century.

Though the Federal Convention was finally called by the Congress under the Articles, the initiative was taken by Hamilton, Madison, and others of the delegates to the Annapolis Convention of 1786, which met to deal with the relatively limited problem of commerce among the central states. Congress authorized the proposed convention to meet "for the sole and express purpose of revising the Articles of Confederation and reporting to Congress" amendments to that document which would render it adequate to "the exigences of Government and the preservation of the Union." Nor did any state authorize its delegates to draft and propose a new constitution.

Had the Federal Convention failed, it would be easy for us to agree that it lacked the authority with which to work out a satisfactory constitution. But if there were handicaps, such as the difficulties of communication and travel vividly described by Albert J. Beveridge in the chapter on "Community Isolation" in his *Life of John Marshall*,[12] and limitations of power, there were also tremendous assets. Some of these are so obvious that they are likely to be overlooked.

Perhaps the greatest asset is the one noted by the late John C. Ranney when he says that "the American Union was based on a remarkably high degree of cultural, social, and political community."[13] A common political and legal tradition was of even more decisive influence than a common language.

There was also a sense of urgency, a conviction that a more effective government was essential to the economic and the international, as well as the domestic political, situation of the United States. To the weakness of the central government were added the fact of an economic depression, and the fears, exaggerated as we know, occasioned by Shay's Rebellion in Massachusetts.

An asset of another kind, but one which should not be overlooked, is that the meetings were secret; there were no reporters, no reports,

---

[12] I, ch. VII.

[13] See his excellent essay, "The Bases of American Federalism," *William and Mary Quarterly*, Third Series, vol. III, no. 1, pp. 1-35.

therefore no speeches to the galleries or to constituents. There was not even an official transcript of the debates, the only comprehensive record we have of the discussions being an unofficial but remarkably careful one kept by James Madison.

The convention was small. Seventy-four delegates were appointed by the state legislatures, but only fifty-five attended and only forty-two remained to the last session, of which number thirty-nine signed the Constitution. There were never more than fifty present at any one meeting. Since the Convention followed the practice of all previous conventions or congresses in America and voted by states, each state having one vote, there could never be more than twelve votes cast, Rhode Island not being represented. In fact, never more than eleven were cast, since the New Hampshire delegates did not arrive until late in July, and by that time two of the three New York delegates had gone home in disgust with the proceedings, and the one remaining delegate, Hamilton, could not cast the vote of that state.

If the Convention had few members, it included several of the foremost Americans, as well as an exceptional proportion of men of ability and experience. The most famous of living Americans were Washington and Franklin; both were present. Washington was elected President of the Convention; his enormous prestige was probably essential to the success of the Convention and to the ratification of its Constitution. The men who carried a disproportionate share of leadership in the Convention were less well known, not only than Washington and Franklin, but also than John Adams and Thomas Jefferson, who were representing their country in London and Paris respectively. Fortunately, some of the best known orators, Patrick Henry among them, were not elected or refused to serve. Quieter, abler men, James Madison and James Wilson in particular, were able to exercise an influence which their knowledge of the needs of the country, as well as their genuine learning in government and law, and their intellectual qualities, fully justified. This would probably not have been the case had it been a forum in which ringing oratory was appreciated at its dramatic, rather than its true, value.

At a time when relatively few went to college, no less than twenty-nine of the fifty-five who attended the Philadelphia Convention were college men. That is a statistic which indicates, among other things, that the delegates generally came from the middle or upper middle and upper classes. Thirty-nine of the delegates had served in the Congress of the Confederation, and at least that many in state legislatures. They knew from their own experience a great deal about the needs of the country and the difficulties of carrying on a central government under the existing system.

The Convention was scheduled to meet on the second Monday in May, but it was not until May 25 that delegates from seven states reached Philadelphia and a quorum was secured. The Convention, or its committees were continually in session from May 25 to September 17, 1787, more than three and one-half months.

A brief outline of events in the Convention may be helpful in following the discussion of agreement and disagreement. The Virginia Plan, written largely by Madison, was introduced on May 29 and was the subject of debate for two weeks. This plan from the delegation representing the largest state contained the startling proposal of a new constitution giving unprecedented powers to the central government. On June 15 the New Jersey, or Small State Plan, was presented. It called for a revised Articles of Confederation. On June 18 Hamilton presented his plan and defended it in a long and brilliant speech, to which the delegates apparently listened with admiration for his eloquence. After he had concluded they went on with their business as though he had not spoken.

After a month of discussion and frequently heated debate, the Convention accepted the Great Compromise. After ten days more of discussion, on July 26, a Committee on Detail was appointed and to it were referred twenty-three resolutions on which agreement had not been reached. That Committee reported on August 6, and its report was debated for five weeks. On September 10 the Committee on Style was appointed. It, with Gouverneur Morris as principal draftsman, took only two days to give virtually final form and language to the proposed Constitution. After a few more days of debate and voting, the Convention passed its final vote on September 17, thirty-nine of the delegates signed the proposed Constitution, and the Convention adjourned.

I have suggested that the greatest asset of the Federal Convention was a basic agreement which existed before the delegates arrived in Philadelphia. Yet it is evident that they disagreed about many things, that they debated and argued, and frequently compromised their differences, over a period of almost four months. This is something short of immediate agreement, and definitely not the fastest or smoothest example of constitution-drafting in American history. There is, as many have read, the well known remark, one quoted with approval by Max Farrand who spent years in editing the best edition we have of the records of the Federal Convention, that the Constitution is a "bundle of compromises."[14]

No one could possibly defend the proposition that the Constitution does not embody a considerable number of compromises. The question is whether this sweeping statement is an accurate and meaningful interpretation of what took place in the Federal Convention. Few of the hundreds who have written about that remarkable group have attempted to draw discriminating conclusions about the nature and basic reasons for agreement and disagreement during its meetings. Among the most interesting and useful generalizations I have discovered are those found in Robert Livingston Schuyler's little book, *The Constitution of the United States*. He concluded that "the disputes in the Convention, the occasions for compromise, were many, but most of them arose over questions essentially political. If one approaches the work of the Convention from the point of view of government and political science, he will naturally be impressed by its compromises. But on the great economic questions at issue between debtor and creditor, farmer and merchant, there was little need for compromise, for there was little disagreement among the delegates."[15] The distinctions between political and economic disagreement and agreement suggests the possibility of an analysis more inclusive, as well as more incisive, than the customary one-sentence generalization.

In my analysis of this problem I shall first deal with disagreement and compromise, and then discuss the nature and importance of agreement. A discussion of disagreement and compromise may properly begin with the first and major obstacle to the success of the Convention, the issue of representation in Congress. The Convention was the last time in American history when the large states were lined up on one

---

[14] *The Framing of the Constitution of the United States*, p. 201. The first three volumes of Farrand's *Records of the Federal Convention* were published in 1911. The fourth, which followed in 1937, contains relatively few additions of importance, but it has a much more useful comprehensive index.

[15] *Op. cit.*, pp. 111-112.

side and the small states on the other. The latter group, or most of
them, insisted on equality of representation in Congress so that each
state would, as in the Stamp Act Congress, the First and Second Continental Congresses, and the Congress under the Articles of Confederation, have an equal vote. To us this division seems largely artificial,
but it reflected strongly held views in 1787. For a time the disagreement over it threatened to disrupt the Convention. Out of that disagreement came the major compromise by which equality of representation was provided for the Senate, while in the House the states were
to be represented in accordance with their population. After this compromise had been adopted the large state, small state line-up disap-
peared, only to reappear briefly when the problem of electing a President came up. Of course the equality of representation in the Senate,
according to which at the present time New York and Nevada each
have two senators, has been an important factor in American history,
as in the decades preceding the Civil War, but the basis of division has
rarely, if ever, been the size of the states.

Another issue relating to representation in Congress was involved
in the counting of slaves. Those states in which there were many slaves
wished them to be counted for purposes of representation. The result
of this particular disagreement was the provision that three-fifths of the
slaves shall be counted. So close a student of the Convention as Professor Schuyler argues that the three-fifths clause was "not the result
of a compromise," because "there was nothing new about it."[16] It is
true that the principle of counting three-fifths of the slaves had been
found in an amendment proposed to the Articles of Confederation and
the same principle was proposed in the New Jersey Plan. But it is also
true that this is an issue on which members of the Convention disagreed, and that the three-fifths ratio was a compromise between those
who wished to have slaves counted and those who wished to have them
not counted. Had they been a little more logical, perhaps they would
have agreed on a fifty-fifty division, but they simply took over the three-
fifths ratio as it had been proposed under the Articles.

The qualifications for voting was a subject over which there was
disagreement in the Convention, some delegates favoring a property
qualification, others being opposed. The Convention decided to leave

16 *The Constitution of the United States*, p. 103.

the regulation of the suffrage to the several states, largely because there were such varying regulations among them. The tendency during and after the Revolution was toward liberalizing the suffrage, a tendency with which the Federal Convention did not attempt to interfere, much less to block. There was apparently no serious disagreement when the delegates decided not to follow the example of most of the states and to require neither property nor religious qualifications for office holding.

One of the clearest examples we have of disagreement and compromise concerns the term of office of members of both houses of Congress. The terms finally agreed upon, two years for members of the House and six for members of the Senate, were clearly the results of compromises, since almost everything was proposed at one time or another, from a one-year term for Representatives, to a life term for Senators.

In view of the important part played in the calling of the Convention by the weakness of the government under the Articles and its inability to carry on the ordinary functions of government, it is surprising how little time was devoted to the discussion, except perhaps in committees, of whose proceedings we have no record, of the powers granted to Congress. The Virginia Plan contained an extremely broad and general grant of powers. There was some discussion of this proposal with indications of disagreement, but the enumeration of the powers of Congress, largely as we find it in the Constitution today, came from the Committee on Detail. A few of the powers proposed, either by that Committee or by individual members of the Convention, were voted down, e.g., the power to issue charters of incorporation, and the power to emit bills of credit, but otherwise opposition to specific powers of Congress was largely in terms of sectional or regional jealousies and fears.

The power to regulate commerce, together with the power to levy customs duties, seems to have been generally accepted, but the delegates from South Carolina and Georgia were bitterly opposed to allowing Congress to regulate, perhaps to abolish, the slave trade. All of the southern states were opposed to the imposition of any tax on exports, since the agrarian South was then the principal exporting area of the country. A majority of the states seems to have been in favor of allowing Congress to abolish the slave trade, but the three southern states indicated that they would stay out of the union if such a power were entrusted to Congress. As a result Congress was prohibited from forbidding the importation of slaves before 1808, and was permitted to impose a tax on "such importation, not exceeding ten dollars for each person." The Congress was also forbidden to impose export taxes. The South won on both of these issues.

On the regulation of foreign commerce or, to use the term most frequently employed in the Convention, "navigation laws," the South wanted protection against regulations which would discriminate against that section, and tried to secure adoption of a requirement that such statutes could be enacted only by a two-thirds vote of both houses of Congress. This they failed to obtain; on this part of the general question of the regulation of commerce the South lost.

The southern states were also fearful of discriminatory action by the Congress when it came to the levying of direct taxes. The term "direct tax" in 1787 apparently did not include income taxes but was rather thought of as limited to taxes on land measured by area and on persons by number. The compromise here was similar to the compromise on counting slaves in representation. Direct taxes were prohibited unless they were apportioned among the states by population, counting three-fifths of the slaves for this purpose.

When the Virginia Plan was introduced it was made clear that the representatives from that powerful state wished to give to the national Congress the power to veto all laws "contravening in the opinion of the National Legislature the articles of Union." That is in sharp contrast with the system then existing, though it has a clear similarity to the power exercised by the Board of Trade over the several colonial legislatures. It is, however, less extreme than Hamilton's proposal that the veto be vested in the governors of the states, since the governors were to be appointed by the national government. Hamilton's suggestion was not seriously considered, but the provision of the Virginia Plan was reported out favorably by the Committee on the Whole. By that time, however, more anti-nationalist representatives were present and it soon became evident that the Virginia proposal was not acceptable to many of the delegates. It is one of the paradoxes of the Federal Convention that the Supreme Law clause of Article VI, which has, at least since the time of Chief Justice Marshall, been generally recognized as one of the bulwarks of national power, originated in the New Jersey Plan and was inserted in the Constitution after being re-proposed on July 17 by Luther Martin of Maryland. Luther Martin was one of those most opposed to centralization; he refused to agree with the Constitution as drafted and he was among the most ardent and most vocal of Anti-Federalists. But when he proposed the Supreme Law clause on July 17, it was agreed to without debate or opposition. Much later, on August 23, Pinckney proposed a legislative veto, one requiring a two-thirds vote of Congress, but this lost by a vote of five states to six.

Contrary to some uninformed opinion about the Convention, there was no debate over the broad issue which became so important in the latter part of the nineteenth century and is among the central issues of the present day, laissez-faire versus collectivism. They neither debated, accepted, nor rejected individualism, the welfare state, or socialism.

The sections of the Constitution dealing with the national legislative body were not the only ones which were the basis for differences of opinion and for compromises. A number of the provisions relating to the executive department of the government, most of which are to be found in Article II of the Constitution, were debated and several are the result of compromises. The clearest instance of this is to be found in the numerous discussions and votes relating to the election of the President.

It will be remembered that the Articles of Confederation provided for no national executive as we understand that term. There was a President of Congress, but he was little more than a presiding officer of the legislative branch. There was also a Committee of the States but it and other committees were not independent of the Congress. There was of course no precedent for the election of an executive. It was quickly agreed in the Convention that there should be a separate executive, but it took them more than three months to agree upon a method of election.

If there was no national executive under the Articles of Confederation, there were separate executives in all of the states, one-man executives in all except Pennsylvania. Only three of the states (New York, Massachusetts, and New Hampshire) provided for popular election of the governor. In the others the state executive was elected by the state legislature. It is therefore not surprising that the Virginia Plan called for election of the national executive by Congress. That seemed the most obvious method, as well as the one in accordance with the practice in three-fourths of the states. That principle of election was generally favored during most of the summer, and on at least one occasion it seems to have been approved by unanimous vote of the states present. Nevertheless, the delegates had doubts about it and when, on August 31, a committee consisting of one delegate from each state was appointed to deal with parts of the Constitution not acted on or postponed, the method of electing the President was one of the problems submitted to it. Apparently one of the reasons why there had been something less than complete agreement was that the smaller states wanted equality of voting in the selection of the President. This committee reported out our curious method of electing a President. It combines features from almost all of the proposals made up to that time, though it is also to be said that it is very similar to a proposal made nearly three months earlier by James Wilson. This compromise plan provided for election by an electoral college, the state legislatures to decide on the method by which the electors were to be selected in each state, the number of electors to be equal to the number of representatives in the House and Senate combined. If no candidate should receive a majority of the votes cast, something which the Founding Fathers thought would be frequently the case, the Senate was to elect from the five candidates standing highest, or from the top two if they were tied, both having a majority, as was possible under a system according to which each elector would vote for two candidates, one of whom could not be a citizen of the elector's state. On the floor of the Convention this system was slightly changed, the principal alteration being that a runoff election would take place in the House rather than the Senate, but, as a concession to the small states, each state would have a single vote.

The Convention went along happily for over three months without anyone suggesting that the country needed a Vice President. That office was proposed by the committee which offered the compromise method of electing the President and, when a question was raised about the need for a Vice President, there was but a single answer, that the committee introduced this office "for the sake of a valuable mode of election which requires two to be chosen at the same time." This answer was based upon the assumption that the electors would vote, to the extent possible, for favorite sons of their own states. But it remains a strange reason for the introduction of an officer given but one

Gouverneur Morris wanted an even stronger executive than did Madison, or than did the majority of the delegates.

The powers allocated to the executive were the result of much discussion and some compromises. There were also a number of proposals which were simply voted down, with no resulting compromises. The absolute veto, for example, was proposed at least three times, but was always defeated. The committee report which proposed the compromise method of electing the President, increased the powers of that officer by adding the authority to negotiate treaties and to make important appointments with the advice and consent of the Senate. The change meant a considerable increase of executive authority; previously both powers had been assigned to the Senate alone. The committee also inserted the provision which is the sole constitutional basis for the Cabinet, that the President could require the opinions in writing of the heads of the several departments.

This survey of the work of the Convention supports Professor Schuyler's interpretation in part, but only in part. It is true that "the disputes in the Convention, the occasions for compromise, were many, but most of them arose over questions essentially political." Moreover, the absence of any lengthy or serious dispute over the prohibitions upon state power contained in Section 10 of Article I—those prohibiting the states from coining money, emitting bills of credit, making anything but gold and silver coin a tender in payment of debts, or passing any law impairing the obligation of contracts—supports his view that the "economic questions at issue between debtor and creditor" were not the basis for prolonged dispute or for compromise.

There is room to question, however, his statement that the economic questions at issue between "farmer and merchant" were not the subject of dispute and compromise. Disputes of this kind in the Convention were largely sectional in nature, and most of the disagreements and resulting compromises between the delegates from the southern states and those representing the northern states were more economic than political. These include such questions as the slave trade, the direct taxation of land and of slaves, the regulation of foreign commerce and the imposition of export duties. To use a classification which I employed some years ago in analyzing the political philosophy of the *Federalist,* the economic differences in the Convention reflected vertical

duty, that of presiding over the Senate, and, if I may q
Vice President Marshall, a single obligation, that of inquiri
about the health of the President, since the compromise pla
for the succession of the Vice President to "the powers a
the said office" when that office becomes vacant "in case
moval of the President from office, or of his death, resign
ability to discharge the powers and duties of the said office

So long as the delegates were of the opinion that the Presi
be elected by Congress, they favored a single term, probal
years. Apparently they were afraid that he would be depe
Congress if he had to look to the Congress for re-election.
acceptance of the compromise method for the election of th
the term was changed to one of four years and nothing wa
re-eligibility.

The views concerning the relation of the President to
varied from that expressed by Roger Sherman on June 1
pressed by Alexander Hamilton on June 18. Neither of
at all representative of the Convention. Sherman said, "He
the Executive Magistracy as nothing more than an institutio
ing the will of the Legislature into effect, that the person
ought to be appointed by and accountable to the Legislature
was the depositary of the supreme will of the Society." It
if anyone, except perhaps Franklin, agreed with this view,
man changed his mind during the course of the summer.

The other extreme is found in Hamilton's plan and spee
wished a "supreme executive authority" to be vested in a si
who shall be elected "to serve during good behavior," i.e.,
unless earlier removed, this executive to be elected by elect
by the people in election districts. In addition to having life
executive would exercise great independent power, includin
lute veto over acts of Congress.

The most representative point of view and the one which w
to that accepted by the Convention, was expressed at var
by James Madison. It may be noted that both James W

---

[17] On this and other issues related to the separation of powers see
"The Origins of the Separation of Powers in America," *Economica*
May, 1933, pp. 169-185.

rather than horizontal cleavages;[18] they were not between the bourgeoisie and the proletariat but rather between rival bourgeois, usually sectional, interests.

ıt ıs difficult to see the extent of the agreement in the Convention unless it is looked at in the light of comparative history. One must step outside of the Convention and consider not so much the day-to-day debates, as the principles and answers which they took for granted and rarely discussed.

Most significant of all the questions which might have been debated, but were not, was the principle of representative government. There was only one man in the Convention who spoke in favor of anything other than popular government as then understood, and that was Alexander Hamilton. But if Hamilton, in his speech of June 18, believed "that the British Government was the best in the world: and that he doubted much whether anything short of it would do in America," no other member of the Convention supported this plea for monarchy and hereditary privilege, nor did anyone propose holding elections other than at regular, fixed intervals. The system of ministerial responsibility and of elections following the loss of a majority in the Commons was imperfectly understood in England and either not understood or not approved in America. Moreover, from the beginning of the Convention, it seems to have been accepted by nearly all delegates present, even though some of the small state groups for a time apparently favored election by the state legislatures, that the lower House of the Federal Congress should be elected by popular vote. In the entire history of federal government there had never been a central legislative body elected by popular vote, certainly not in America where the Congress had been elected by the state legislatures. The small state group seems not to have opposed popular election of the lower House, but rather to have supported equal voting power for the small states. After the Great Compromise no voice was raised against the principle of popular election. The delegates did not support popular election for the Senate or for the national executive or for the courts, but then it is to be remembered that nothing of this kind was found in the central government, that the upper houses in several states were elected by the lower,

---

[18] "The Federalist on the Nature of Political Man," *Ethics*, LIX, January 1949, no. 2, Part II, pp. 1-31.

and that state judges were appointed by the governors or the legislatures.

The delegates unanimously assumed that there should be a written constitution with an amending clause. In the twentieth century virtually all countries follow that assumption; in the eighteenth century the Americans were almost unique among the nations in so doing.

The new government was then to be republican and it was to be based upon a written constitution which was fundamental law, one which could be changed by a special process. It was also to be far stronger, with many more effective powers, than the government under the Articles of Confederation. Even the New Jersey Plan extended the power to tax and to regulate commerce. It is evident that from the beginning of the debates, though there were disagreements over particulars, every member of the Convention agreed that the central government should be more powerful. Some of the most important powers given to Congress by the Committee on Detail, which drafted the section enumerating the delegated powers, were accepted without debate. The principal differences of opinion, though not the only ones, were related to sectional issues.

It is of the greatest significance that the Convention accepted the principle that the central government should legislate for and tax individual persons. This, like the principle of popular election of the House and of representation in that body according to population, is a break with the history of federal government up to 1787. Before that time federal government had meant a league or confederation of sovereign or quasi-sovereign states, the central government having authority to deal with states but not with individual citizens. It should also be remembered, however, that the delegates did not agree with the principle of straight nationalism as Hamilton proposed. They accepted a mixed form, a new system combining nationalism and federalism. Since 1787 the term federal has come to mean a mixed system of this kind, the old kind of federalism usually being called a confederation.

Two of the most significant clauses, so far as the nature of this new or American federalism is concerned, are the supreme law clause and the necessary and proper clause which was inserted by the Committee on Detail. Neither of these clauses was the subject of debate.

Though there were numerous questions relating to the distribution of powers and to the relation of the Congress and the President, there was almost no dispute over the principle that the new government should be one in which there should be a separation of powers with its correlative principle, checks and balances.[19] The point of view expressed by Roger Sherman early in the Convention was not debated, any more than was Hamilton's plan which would have vested a much larger share of power than was acceptable to the other delegates in the executive. This is one of the numerous subjects on which there was substantial and general agreement, though there were differences of opinion and frequent compromises on matters of detail.

Except for Franklin and one or two other delegates, unicameralism had no support in the Convention. To be sure the New Jersey Plan called for a unicameral legislature, but that was for the purpose of securing equality of voting power to the small states. When the Great Compromise was accepted, no more was heard of unicameralism. The delegates, with almost no exceptions, believed in bicameralism for the central government as they did for the states, and for the same reason, the distrust of unchecked power in any assembly, plus the need to give representation to the small states in the Senate. The statement sometimes made that the Senate is "a happy accident" is misleading. The principle that each state has the same number of representatives is the result of a compromise, though perhaps not the happiest of compromises or accidents, but bicameralism was the accepted principle from the beginning, as is made plain in the Virginia Plan and the early acceptance of that principle in it.

Similarly, from the beginning nearly all of the delegates agreed that there should be a single, rather than a plural, executive. Virtually all of the states had single executives and almost all of the delegates, even most of those from Pennsylvania which had a plural executive, assumed and preferred a single President to anything corresponding to the British Ministry.

One of the major innovations was that the central government should have, not just one court of appeals, but a separate judicial system. That, like the popular election of the House and the authority of the central government to impose taxes and regulations directly upon individuals, was a new feature in a federal government. There was, how-

---

[19] See my article cited above, "The Origins of the Separation of Powers in America," pp. 180-183.

ever, greater differences of opinion over this point than over the other innovations just mentioned. After some debate, the Virginia proposal that Congress shall establish a system of lower courts was voted down by a vote of five states to three. When the motion was amended so that Congress could establish a system of lower courts, but was not required to do so, the proposal was accepted by the somewhat surprising majority of eight to two. Life tenure for the judges of the federal courts seems to have been assumed from the beginning.

Such were the agreements and disagreements of 1787. It is true, as Professor Schuyler and others have argued, that there were disputes and occasions for compromise over political questions. It is also true that the compromises were impressive. But far more impressive were the major assumptions upon which there was no need for compromise. The most fundamental political or constitutional issues were taken for granted without debate, or they were only briefly discussed. These include such basic issues as representative government, elections at fixed intervals, a written constitution which is a supreme law and which contains an amending clause, separation of powers and checks and balances, a bicameral legislature, a single executive, and a separate court system. These principles could have been taken for granted in no other country in the eighteenth century, nor could they in combination have been accepted in any other country even after discussion and vote. The nature and extent of this basic agreement throws far more light upon the political and constitutional thought of Americans in 1787 than do the disputes over questions which were nearly always matters of detail, or which were based largely upon sectional disagreement, or upon the size of the several states.

To put the matter another way: if Alexander Hamilton had had a dozen followers in the Convention, instead of none, or if Paine had been there and had had a group of sympathizers, there would have been far more disagreement over political and constitutional issues. Had both Hamilton and Paine been present and been supported by other delegates, the polarization of philosophies which would very likely have resulted might have made lasting agreement improbable, perhaps impossible. It is when we contrast the debates and the decisions of the Federal Convention with those of comparable bodies in many other countries that we see how great was the area of agreement and how essential it was to the lasting success of the Convention's work.

If this point of view seems exaggerated, I suggest that one recall the history of the struggle over such questions in other countries of modern times. In Philadelphia, monarchy, feudalism, and hereditary privilege were not issues. The delegates did not have to resolve the conflicting claims of church and state. Nor was there in this country such religious cleavage as made the union of all India impossible, when that subcontinent became independent a few years ago. There was no dispute even vaguely comparable to the struggles over capitalism versus communism which have torn countries apart and resulted in civil war and dictatorship during the last four decades. To the Americans of 1787 these fundamental questions were simply not issues.

My first purpose in this chapter has been to indicate the great and determining importance of agreement among the delegates. With a single exception, presently to be considered, virtually all of them held views which were identical, or so nearly so as to make for easy agreement on those basic subjects where lack of agreement has frequently made stable governments according to known and settled laws impossible.

A second, and not insignificant, aim has been to point out that the delegates were able, when they did disagree, to work out acceptable compromises or, more frequently, and just as essential, to accept defeat when outvoted. Had they been too proud, too stiff-necked, too intransigent, either to accept defeat when on the losing side, or unwilling to compromise their differences, the Convention would very likely have gone down in history as one of the many failures in the attempt to establish a workable and a lasting government. Fortunately for their posterity, the point of view which was accepted by most, though not by all of them, was that expressed feelingly by Benjamin Franklin on the last day of the Convention meetings, when the final draft, having been read, was before them for a vote. The aged Doctor urged that everyone who had remained to the last session sign the Constitution. He freely admitted that he did not agree with all of its provisions, but said that experience had taught him to doubt his own first judgments. More than once he had changed "opinions even on important subjects." He doubted whether another convention could "make a better constitution." It too would consist of men with prejudices, passions, local interests and errors of judgment, as well as wisdom. He asked that each of his colleagues who had objections to the Constitution "would with me, on this occasion doubt a little of his own infallibility, and . . . put his name to this instrument."

Franklin's speech must have been the more impressive to the delegates who knew that he had been outvoted on a number of issues and that his point of view had, on others, been ignored.

Doubtless it is unnecessary to labor the point that without agreement on certain fundamental questions a stable, constitutional government is impossible, and that without the willingness to accept a majority vote or, alternatively, to compromise differences, a government of laws will not long endure. The validity of these generalizations is supported by the results of the failure of the Convention to solve one great question, or pair of questions—slavery and the slave trade. No action was possible on the first, and the second was simply brushed under the rug, there to remain for twenty years.

Slavery existed in almost all of the states at that time. There was some anti-slavery sentiment, reflected in the Convention by Gouverneur Morris who said it is "a nefarious institution, . . . the curse of heaven on the States where it prevails," and by George Mason who spoke feelingly of the miserable effects of slavery on slave owners and poor alike and virtually prophesied "national calamities" if the institution should be continued and the slave area expanded. But the opposition to slavery at that time was not sufficiently general to permit either agreement or compromise on its abolition. Even that abominable traffic, the slave trade, could not be abolished. The southernmost states, to their later impoverishment and humiliation, threatened not to join the Union if power to prohibit the slave trade were given to Congress. On this point they were adamant.

The existence of slavery, its spread westward, the rise of burning opposition to it, together with the intransigence of the effective majority in the South and Southwest, eventually led to war. On that question, and only on that question, there was disagreement beyond the possibility either of submission to the vote of a majority, or of compromise. We have in that story the perfect, and tragic, example of the failure of constitutional methods. This failure serves to throw into clearer relief the extent to which there was a tremendous, and essential, area of agreement in the Convention, together with the ability either to compromise or to accept majority vote on issues where agreement was less than complete.

Ours has indeed been a fortunate, or a wise, and certainly a happier, country because the great issues which have divided us, have, with the single exception of slavery, been resolved without recourse to war. On most such issues the minority has accepted the decision of the majority. Others, many others, have been compromised.

I would not want to be understood as saying that all issues or principles can or should be compromised, or that the majority is always correct and the minority should always accept its decision. There are principles and issues which cannot be compromised; there are times when majority vote does not give a final answer. But history contains so many examples of an absolute conviction of self-rightness being founded on fanaticism and ignorance, of eternal principles which were no more than transitory policies, that the tolerant humility of Franklin seems the way of maturity and wisdom. If men could but agree on both aims and means, there would be few problems of politics to plague and divide us. So long as men remain prone to selfishness and emotion and fallible in judgment, a decent respect for the opinions of others and a willingness to compromise are essential to the continuance of constitutional government.

III. WAS THE CONSTITUTION REACTIONARY?

The Centennial of the Constitution was the occasion for an outburst of oratory and comparable writing in which the orators and authors sometimes seemed to have confused the work of the Convention of 1787 with the Tables handed down from Sinai, or at least with writings which had their origin on Olympus. As one reads some of these magniloquent statements he gets the impression that the authors of the Constitution were divinely inspired patriots of unsurpassed wisdom in whose work there is to be found no human flaw.

At about the same time we find the beginnings of a point of view, shortly to be widely accepted by twentieth century historians and political scientists, which is in almost complete contrast with the attitude of pious patriotism. According to this view the Constitution was the product of a reactionary movement engineered by the selfish rich; it is, therefore, an anti-democratic document, skillfully designed to secure the blessings of liberty only to the prosperous and the predatory.

Both of these views, though commonly in somewhat less extravagant form, are still to be found in writings and speeches. The first of them is interesting as a species of folklore or an example of zeal for popular favor, but those who express such views proceed "without fear and without research" and with scant attempt to document their conclusions. It is not a particularly profitable point of view to make the basis for scholarly analysis. The other and almost antithetical view is a much better point of departure for an examination of the nature of the American Constitution.

This interpretation seems to have had its latter-day origin (for it is also to be found in some of the writings and speeches of the ratification controversy) in the Populist and early progressive movements during the last two decades of the nineteenth century. That was a time when the states were extending their regulatory statutes over a good many aspects of the American economy, and the first period in which the national Congress made serious attempts to regulate business enterprise, particularly the railroads and the trusts. It is also the period in which labor controversies became burning issues, and in which the income tax, previously sustained by the Supreme Court of the United States, was held to be unconstitutional. A number of Supreme Court decisions, some applying to state, some to Congressional legislation, seemed to many persons to put the Constitution solidly behind the rich and powerful. Critics of the Court drew the conclusion that these decisions demonstrated the undemocratic and restrictive nature of the Constitution. They seemed, that is to say, to read the point of view of the Supreme Court of the 1890's back into the attitude of the Framers of 1787. A few quotations from serious scholarly writings may illustrate how far this point of view was carried, as well as serve as the basis for an examination of the nature of the Constitution.

In 1903 the late Charles E. Merriam published his first little textbook, *History of American Political Theories,* in which the following sentences are to be found:

> "After independence from Great Britain had been won and formally recognized, two broad tendencies appear during the formative period of the Union,—the reactionary and radical. The theory of the first party is well expressed in the Constitution itself, in the *Federalist,* and in the writings of John Adams and Alexander Hamilton. The theory of the radical element is best stated by Thomas Jefferson, the central figure in the practical politics as in the political philosophy of the democratic school."[20]

The view expressed by Merriam was rapidly accepted by textbook writers. That tendency was accelerated four years later when Professor J. Allen Smith of the University of Washington published his *Spirit of American Government.* In this book, which was to be widely read and adopted by historians and political scientists, the ideas stated briefly by Merriam and others were developed at considerable length. Rather than quote from the book itself, let me quote from a significant article about Smith and his book in the *Encyclopedia of the Social Sciences,* published in 1934, twenty-seven years after Smith's book appeared. The article is by William Seagle, an assistant editor of the *Encyclopedia.* Seagle says that J. Allen Smith was the first to demonstrate that the Constitution was a reactionary document, and that Smith not merely stated but gave conclusive evidence to support the view that "Its mechanisms were intended to make majority rule impossible while preserving its external forms. This end the Fathers had accomplished not only by means of the judicial veto and the adoption of an exceedingly rigid amending process but by working out a highly intricate system of checks and balances." The Constitution was far from

---

[20] *History of American Political Theories,* p. 96.

welcome to the people at large and was ratified only "as the result of the guile and pressure on the part of the conservative business interests whose influence had preponderated in the drafting of the instrument." Mr. Seagle concludes that Smith's "fundamental thesis remains unshakable. Beard's *Economic Interpretation of the Constitution,* published six years later . . . was hardly more than a documentation of Smith's general conclusions."[21]

Beard's *Economic Interpretation* was one of the most influential historical books published in this century. Beard's conclusions are extremely difficult to pin down, particularly in relation to the charge that the Constitution was reactionary. The views attributed to Beard by Seagle and many others are more clearly expressed in another extremely influential book, Charles and Mary Beard's *The Rise of American Civilization,* which appeared in 1927. There we find these distinguished authors, when dealing with the Federal Convention, saying that "equally general was the conviction that the states should not be allowed to issue bills of credit or impair the obligation of contracts. Almost unanimous was the opinion that democracy was a dangerous thing, to be restrained, not encouraged, by the Constitution, to be given as little voice as possible in the new system, to be hampered by checks and balances."[22]

That same point of view is many times restated in textbooks on history and political science, and in such very widely read and influential works as V. L. Parrington's *Main Currents in American Thought.*[23] It is interesting, and of some significance for an interpretation of the whole of Parrington's three volumes, that he was a close friend of J. Allen Smith and his *Main Currents* was dedicated to Smith's memory.

The point of view expressed by such scholars as the Beards and Parrington was reiterated by many others, sometimes with slight variations, as for example the statement in *The Triumph of American Capitalism* by Professor Louis M. Hacker of Columbia University. In 1940 he wrote that "if the thought of any single individual dominated them [the members of the Convention] it was Alexander Hamilton's."[24] He goes on to add that "The numerous majority—'the turbulence and

21 *Encyclopedia of the Social Sciences,* vol. XIV, p. 116.
22 I, p. 315.
23 I, p. 282.
24 p. 186.

follies of democracy' of which Edmund Randolph spoke—was to be curbed at all costs."

This general attitude continues to be widely accepted and reproduced. It necessarily involves the doctrine that the drafting and adoption of the Federal Constitution meant a break in the continuity of the movement for popular government which was carried forward during the Revolution. For, according to this interpretation of our history, the Constitution was reactionary and therefore not in the line of continuous growth. The adoption of the Constitution meant a set-back, a retrogression from which the development of democracy did not begin to recover until the victory of Jefferson in 1800. It is a view which is eminently worth careful examination, particularly so in a study attempting to place the essential elements of continuity in American constitutional history of the Revolutionary and Constitutional periods.

There is but a single route by which one can proceed toward that goal: the analysis of the Constitution, and of the principles embodied in it, in relation to the ideas and institutions which had been adopted or generally accepted in America during the preceding eleven years. That statement may appear so truistic as to take its place among the most unnecessary academic platitudes. Curiously, and unhappily for our understanding of the past, it is the one procedure which has rarely been employed. Five or six other methods of ascertaining an answer, or of predetermining an answer, to the question, Was the Constitution reactionary? have been employed from time to time. They throw more light upon the point of view of those who have employed them than upon the nature of the Constitution at the time of its drafting and adoption, but they call for some mention, since they have, singly or collectively, been used by many scholars and popularizers.

One of the most common has been that of judging features of the Constitution by ideas or institutions accepted in this country several generations later. The Constitution was written in 1787, not in 1828 or 1887, and the comparisons must be those of its time. Even this method has been used with such selectivity as to ignore the continued popularity of the separation of powers and checks and balances, and to emphasize the fact that the Framers did not remove the restrictions then existing on the suffrage.

A second popular method has been that of assessing the motives of the Framers. Almost all of us engage in this kind of activity when discussing our contemporaries, though we ordinarily realize that we are taking part in a guessing game when we do so. To make the answer to a serious problem of historiography depend upon the assignment of possible motives, when we seldom if ever have reliable evidence, is to substitute gossip for scholarly method.

A more respectable but still unreliable procedure has been that of listing those who were for and those who were against the Constitution, or, much more frequently, of listing two or three leading Federalists and then contrasting their point of view with one or more well known Anti-Federalists. Thus Alexander Hamilton is frequently listed as the archtype of Federalist, only a few months ago as "the architect of the new government,"[25] and his point of view is assigned to the Constitution, while presumptive democrats such as Patrick Henry are cited as opponents. This procedure ignores, among other things, such essential and positive evidence as that Hamilton's influence on the decisions in the Convention was slight and that he frankly said, on the last day of the Convention, when urging the other delegates to sign the Constitution, as something which was better than the Articles, that "no man's ideas were more remote from the plan than his own were known to be."

In the course of discussions proceeding along this line we are frequently informed that Jefferson was critical of the new Constitution. He undoubtedly was critical of several provisions of the proposed document when he first received a copy of it in the fall of 1787. He deplored the absence of a complete bill of rights and he was disturbed by the unlimited re-eligibility of the President. On the other hand, he was far less critical of the proposed Constitution than many of those in the Convention who favored ratification, Hamilton included, and, a little over a year later, on March 18, 1789, in a letter to David Humphreys, he wrote that "the Constitution . . . is unquestionably the wisest ever yet presented to men."[26] This statement was made after he had had time to consider the document fully and to correspond with some of his friends in this country about it.

If we continue this process of lining up prominent figures on one

<hr />

25 In the review, in the *New York Times Book Review*, April 7, 1957, of Broadus Mitchell, *Alexander Hamilton*, 1755-1788. Professor Mitchell's claims for Hamiltonian influences in the Convention are more moderate. See ch. 24.

26 *Writings* (Ford ed.), V, p. 89.

side or the other and drawing conclusions from the division, we run across such oddities as that Samuel Adams, after some hesitation, supported ratification, though Patrick Henry and Luther Martin were opposed. I find it difficult to see much support for the reactionary thesis in their opposition, inasmuch as both, after the Constitution was established, became ardent and conservative Federalists.

A related, and even more unreliable, procedure, is to quote what one or two members of the Convention said during the course of the debates in that body. We are frequently informed that Elbridge Gerry, on May 31, when the discussion involved popular election of the House of Representatives, opposed that innovation and said that "The evils we experience flow from an excess of democracy." That statement is quoted without indication that Gerry lost out in his opposition to popular election of the House, and also that he refused to sign the Constitution and was opposed to ratification. It is unusual, in interpretations of this kind, that Franklin is cited as supporting the Constitution, and doing so with a considerable degree of enthusiasm. We know that Franklin was far more sympathetic with the expansion of popular government than Gerry or Randolph, or, for that matter, Henry or Martin.

A fifth approach involves the charge that the Constitution was ratified by skillful maneuverings and machinations of an organized group, presumably a minority of the voters, though not much emphasis is placed upon numbers and proportions, since we lack reliable evidence on this point for most of the states. Doubtless those who were strongly in favor of the new government did maneuver as best they could under the circumstances to secure a favorable vote, and in Pennsylvania they moved with perhaps unseemly speed, but surely concealed manipulations were made difficult by the process of ratification stipulated by the Convention—the selection of delegates at a special election held in each state, when the only issue was the adoption of the proposed Constitution. Attempts to win elections by methods other than appeal to the reasoned and informed judgment of all of the voters did not begin in 1787 nor end in 1788.

A sixth method, and, since the publication of Charles Beard's *Economic Interpretation of the Constitution* in 1913, probably the most substantial of all the defective procedures for deciding the nature of the Constitution in 1787, is that of dealing with the economic interests of the Framers. This approach brings us back very close to the attribution of motives, since it involves drawing conclusions from the economic holdings and status of the Framers, and of some of those who supported ratification, as to their motives and their objectives. This approach has been based upon a simplified and unsophisticated version of economic determinism which assumes, without examination, that the amount and kind of wealth determines the institutional preferences of the persons concerned.

The Framers, and the Federalists generally, had much the same economic and social backgrounds as the authors of the Declaration of Independence, the Articles of Confederation, and most of the state constitutions. This is not a complete answer to the Beardian doctrine though it is relevant, significant, and rarely mentioned. Beard and his followers make much of the fact that a considerable number of the members of the Federal Convention owned federal securities which would increase in value with the adoption of a stronger central government. One difficulty about that statement is that Beard relied for his findings very largely upon Treasury listings of the early 1790's, and we have no way of knowing how many of the men who were listed as holding substantial amounts of federal securities in those years had been owners in 1787 or 1788. This and other serious weaknesses in Beard's scholarly procedures have been subjected to harsh scrutiny in the recent book by Robert E. Brown, *Charles Beard and the Constitution*. There are additional difficulties about Beard's discussions, among them such facts as that not all of the individuals listed as holding federal securities or other personal property, and by no means all of the geographical areas he mentions, seem to vote as could be expected if his assumptions are accepted.[27]

These six methods or procedures, whether employed singly or in combination, do not provide an answer to the question: was the Constitution reactionary in 1787? Of course if we mean by reactionary no more than opposed to, or reacting against the existing frame of government, the Articles of Confederation, we reduce the question to an absurdity. Certainly the Framers were dissatisfied with the Articles and both

---

[27] As Broadus Mitchell points out, *op. cit.*, p. 384, such ardent advocates of ratification as Hamilton, Madison, and Gouverneur Morris had no personal property concern in their work, while such Anti-Federalists among the delegates as Yates, Lansing, Martin, Mason, and Gerry stood to gain in their own estates if the Constitution were adopted.

prepared and supported another document to take its place. In that same sense the American Revolution and the Declaration of Independence are products of reaction against Parliamentary and royal control of the colonies during the preceding ten or twelve years. Similarly, the French Revolution was a reaction against the old régime in France. All revolutions are in this sense reactionary. But I take it that reactionary is used here in the sense of retrogressive, so far as concerns the development of popular government. The Constitution of 1787 was reactionary in 1787 if it was a document which went contrary to the democratic or popular tendencies of the Revolution and the period of the Confederation as those tendencies are exemplified in comparable documents, that is, in the state constitutions and the Articles of Confederation.

There is one preliminary aspect of such an analysis. As already pointed out, some scholars who have characterized the Constitution as reactionary have included as part of the evidence for such a conclusion the argument that the Constitution was drafted and adopted in a less than democratic method, and that it was hastily railroaded through one or two state conventions without time for adequate consideration.

This point might be turned into a question, why were the delegates not elected by vote of the people, and why was the Constitution not submitted to the people for approval or rejection? The answer is simple. The Convention was elected by the state legislatures, which was the only method of selecting delegates to a central or national body ever used in this country. It was the method that had been employed for selection of delegates to the Albany Congress, the Stamp Act Congress, the First and Second Continental Congresses, as well as the Congress under the Articles of Confederation. No other method was seriously proposed, or could possibly have been accepted at that time.

The Constitution was submitted for ratification, not to the state legislatures as had been done during the Revolution when the Articles was ratified but to popularly elected conventions in the States. It may well be that the reason the Framers adopted this new procedure was their distrust of the state legislatures, since many of those bodies were believed to be strongholds of states rights. But whatever the motive the result was the nearest thing to a popular referendum ever known in this country or, for that matter, in the entire history of federal government. The election of delegates to the state conventions was on a ·

single issue, the ratification of the proposed constitution. The suffrage qualifications for voting were those existing under state law at that time, except that in New York all free males were allowed to vote. This procedure was certainly not reactionary.

One of the most common yet farfetched arguments in support of the proposition that the Constitution of 1787 was reactionary is that it went counter to the possibilities of democratic government, meaning, presumably, simple majority rule, in that it contains provisions for the separation of powers, for checks and balances, including judicial review. One has only to read the Anti-Federalist literature of the ratification controversy to find that the opponents of the Constitution generally contended that it would be unsafe to freedom and self-government because it did not contain enough separation of powers and checks and balances. Patrick Henry, for example, argued in the Virginia Convention that judicial review was, as embodied in the Constitution, too weak to protect the rights either of the states or of individual citizens. In the numbers of the *Federalist* devoted to an analysis of the separation of powers in the Constitution (nos. 47-51) Madison is not trying to convince the voters and the delegates to ratifying conventions that the separation of powers and checks and balances are good things, but rather trying to convince them that the Constitution contains these principles in sufficient measure to render it safe.

A fundamental assumption of nearly all political thinking in America at this time was that men in public office are not to be trusted, that human nature is sadly defective, and that institutional provisions must be made to safeguard the governed against the ever present tendency to abuse of powers. This view is found in Anti-Federalist and Federalist literature alike.

So far as one can tell from the debates in the Convention, only two or three members of the Convention, notably Hamilton and Franklin, had doubts about the separation of powers. Franklin apparently desired to vest nearly all governmental power in a unicameral legislature, while Hamilton wanted much power vested in an executive with life tenure. It is interesting that Franklin and Hamilton agreed in opposing a separation of powers, just as Adams and Jefferson agreed in defending separation vigorously.

What the members of the Convention adopted in this respect was what was stated as principle, and in varying measure applied, in the existing state constitutions, particularly in the three constitutions adopted, in New York, Massachusetts and New Hampshire, between 1777 and 1784. Those of Massachusetts and New Hampshire, which contained the clearest application of this principle, were adopted only after statewide referenda, and only after previous attempts at constitution-writing had been rejected by the voters, in large measure because they did not contain a sufficient amount of separation of powers and checks and balances to render them safe.

It is of some significance that the only restriction which the Constitution imposes on the form and structure of the state governments is the guarantee, in Article IV, Section 4, of "a republican form of government." That, to give it its 1787 meaning, was most definitely not a restriction upon the extension of popular rule, as subsequent events proved, but was a guarantee against the establishment in the states of monarchy or hereditary rule such as existed in most European countries at that time.

A closely related part of the argument, if most of the statements that the Constitution was reactionary can be dignified by calling them arguments, is that it did not provide for popular control of the central government. The argument is quite as unhistorical as that which assumes that the acceptance of separation of powers and checks and balances was a sign of opposition to popular government.

Most of the state constitutions provided for popular election of both houses of the legislature, though some provided only for election of the lower house by the voters, the upper house being elected by the lower. In only three states was the governor elected by the voters.

Under the Articles of Confederation no officer of the central government was elected by popular vote, and only the Congress was elected by the state legislatures.

There is a very considerable contrast in this respect as between the Articles of Confederation and the Constitution. Under the new system the representatives were to be elected by popular vote, something new in the history of federal government, the senators by the state legislatures, a continuation of the pre-existing system. The President was to be selected by electors who were to be chosen as the state legislatures should determine. It is evident that the only office, other than the judges of the federal courts, removed from control of the state legislatures was the House of Representatives, and there popular vote was substituted for selection by the state legislatures.

Appointment of the federal judges by the President with the advice and consent of the Senate seems to have been accepted without much discussion in the Convention, doubtless because popular election of judges in the states was not adopted until well into the nineteenth century.

The longer terms of office for Representatives and Senators than was then customary can correctly be cited as evidence of a desire for stability and continuity in office. Annual elections were not, however, universal in the states, as witness the Virginia and New York Senates with four-year terms, and the Maryland Senate with a five-year term.

Some members of the Federal Convention favored including property or other restrictions on the suffrage in the national Constitution, but of course they lost out, even though their words are sometimes quoted in statements on the nature of the Constitution as though these advocates of restrictions on the suffrage had won in the Convention. The Constitution not only imposes no restrictions on voting; it imposes neither property nor religious qualifications for federal offices, though most of the states at that time had either property or religious qualifications, or both, for office holders. This change is an important one and it is directly and entirely in the direction of a wider distribution of political power.

Another curiosity of the general interpretation of the Constitution as reactionary is that it is made difficult to amend. It is, but not when compared with the existing constitution, the Articles of Confederation. If any feature of the Constitution is less restrictive than the comparable rule then in existence it is the amending clause. The change from the requirement of unanimous ratification by the states to the requirement of ratification by three-fourths of the states is one of the important victories for constitutional longevity and adaptability. Perhaps a simpler and easier method of amendment would have been preferable, but, given the circumstances and the jealousies of that day, it seems likely that any device, such as a national referendum, which ignored state lines, or any provision requiring less than a three-fourths majority, would have been unacceptable.

In the statements supporting the proposition that the Constitution was reactionary we find rather less made of the point that this document gave more power to the central government than did the Articles of Confederation, though some have seen in this centralization of power a tendency away from local control, and, therefore, away from popular control. That argument is a confused and confusing one, especially when we recall that most of the democratic revolutions of modern times have resulted in a greater degree of centralization than existed before.

So far as concerns the distribution of powers between states and central government, the Constitution of 1787 carried on the tendency toward a more centralized government which began even before the revolution, and was developed during those years. The government under the Articles was weak, but it was far more centralized than anything known in this country before the Revolution.

To be sure, the wealthy more often favored a stronger central government than did the small farmers, or others living in remote areas, but not all of the wealthy favored centralization nor did all of the democratically inclined men of that era favor a weak central government. Jefferson had criticized the Articles of Confederation in this respect and found no fault with the proposed Constitution so far as centralization of powers was concerned. Fear and distrust of a more centralized governmental system was undoubtedly the chief basis of opposition to the Constitution, but it does not follow that the Constitution was for this reason reactionary.

Another very frequent basis of criticism of the proposed Constitution in 1787 and 1788 was the absence of a bill of rights such as was to be found in most of the state constitutions of that time. Here it is not sufficient to point out that the Articles of Confederation contained no bill of rights, because the government under the Articles lacked the power to deal directly with individual persons. Nor is it sufficient to indicate that some of the state constitutions contained no such guarantees of rights; the principle was generally recognized and accepted in this country at that time.

On this point the Framers, or a majority of them, were curiously inconsistent. Section 9 of Article I contains guarantees of some of the most essential prohibitions in bills of rights (habeas corpus, bills of attainder, ex post facto laws, titles of nobility) and Section 2 of Article III contains two other major guarantees (jury trial in criminal cases and prohibition of bills of attainder, as well as the definition of treason) but, for reasons which are still unclear, the Framers apparently believed that no additional guarantees were necessary, or even relevant. On this point they were confused.

No proposal to have a bill of rights was made in the Convention, unless something was said about it in one of the committees and that seems improbable, until September 12. They had been debating, drafting and voting for over three and a half months before Mason, supported by Gerry, proposed that a bill of rights be attached to the document then taking its final shape. The only speaker to argue against Mason and Gerry was Roger Sherman, who had signed both the Declaration of Independence and the Articles of Confederation. Sherman apparently made a very brief speech in which he said that a bill of rights was not needed, that the state bills of rights were in effect and would be sufficient. He was clearly wrong on this point, but he was supported by a vote of ten states to none against Mason's motion. I shall have some additional comment on this point a little later.

Another, and more substantial basis for the argument that the Constitution was reactionary, is to be found in its provisions concerning the relation of government to economic life. Important qualifications are, however, required in this particular discussion.

As I pointed out in the preceding chapter, there was no debate in the Convention over the great issue of the last three generations, laissez faire versus social control. That issue was to become of primary importance on the national scene a century later; it had not taken form in 1787.

No important person in the United States in 1787 had attacked private property, and the state bills of rights, so far as they contain references to property, are quite clear that the right to own and be protected in the ownership of property was one of the essential rights under a free government. Parrington was confused when he wrote that "The Revolutionary conception of equalitarianism that asserted the rights of man apart from property and superior to property, did not enter into their thinking as a workable hypothesis."[28]

The Constitution prohibits the states from emitting bills of credit, coining money, or making anything but gold or silver a legal tender. It is evident that the Framers were opposed to, reacted against, state issuance and control of money. That same distrust of state legisla-

---

[28] *Main Currents in American Thought,* I, p. 282.

tion relating to money and financial obligations, was made evident in the prohibition imposed upon the states against impairing the obligation of contracts, a clause probably modeled on a similar one in the Ordinance of 1787 for the Northwestern Territories.[29] A provision somewhat related to that prohibition in Article I Section 10, but referring to the national government, is to be found in the first sentence of Article VI, "all debts contracted and engagements entered into, before the adoption of this Constitution, shall be as valid against the United States under this Constitution, as under the Confederation."

A considerable amount of the historical writing of the last half century or more has been based upon a curious pair of assumptions: the men who wrote and voted for the Declaration of Independence and for the state bills of rights and the first state constitutions were great patriots, whereas the men who wrote or voted for the Constitution of 1787 were selfish, economically determined plotters. The Declaration and the state bills of rights were liberating and democratic documents, whereas the later state constitutions, with their greater emphasis upon the separation of powers, and the federal Constitution were intended "to make the country safe from democracy." This dichotomy is evidence of an unhistorical rather than a historical interpretation of our past. It is founded not so much in the history of that time as in the history of a century or more later.

Of course the Founding Fathers sought stability, just as they sought personal security. They found stability and security in the institutional devices and guarantees of the state constitutions, particularly those of New York, Massachusetts and New Hampshire, and their work was in the central line of development, not only of the second half of the eighteenth century but also of the first half of the nineteenth century in this country.

Where were the breaks with the past? Certainly not in the principle of the rule of law or of constitutionalism. Not in the structure of government. Not in the system of elections, though the terms of office were longer than were to be found in most of the states. Not in the amending process, which was liberalized. Not even in the greater centralization of powers in the federal government, since there they were

---

[29] B. F. Wright, *The Contract Clause of the Constitution*, pp. 6-10.

carrying on the tendency which goes back to 1776, if not to 1765. No, they were reflecting the same point of view, as many of them were the same men, of those amazing years of constitution-writing which began in 1776 with the Virginia Constitution.

I hesitate to use the word progressive, since it was not used in this sense at that time and has come to have dubious connotations in recent years, but the extent to which their ideas and institutional devices were foreshadowed by what went before and were continued by what came after might justify the use of that term. At least it is much more accurate than reactionary. For, with the rise of the common man in the first half of the nineteenth century, their work was applauded and continued, not repudiated and reversed. The only changes made in the form of government were matters of detail, such as the Twelfth Amendment, which straightened out the unanticipated problem of the same number of votes for President and Vice President. The Constitution of 1787 made but a shadowy and unclear provision for judicial review of Congressional legislation and this section was not condemned by the Anti-Federalists. The institution of judicial review, which originated in the states, was strengthened in both state and national governments during the period of democratic expansion. Not even the provisions restricting the economic powers of the states were changed. Most of them were reinforced by state action. It is substantially correct to say that the provisions of the Constitution which have been characterized as undemocratic were, with the exception of the section on the slave trade, strengthened in the nineteenth century. Nearly all of the applicable ones were adopted in the popular constitutions of the states.

Since the Framers included some of the most essential provisions customarily found in bills of rights at that time in the Constitution, they should, to be consistent, have included more. Apparently they believed additional guarantees to be unnecessary because the new government was one of enumerated powers and because of the existence of the state bills of rights. It seems likely that they did not fully realize just what they had created in the way of a central government with the power to legislate for individual citizens. At times they understood the implications of the new system, at others they failed to see them clearly. This is not surprising in view of the fact that they had invented a new form of federalism. That they should have understood as fully as they did its nature and its meaning is as astonishing as it is unusual in the history of government.

Only as regards the relation of state governments to economic problems were they what can be called reactionary. They did react against some of the financial and economic legislation of the Revolution and the period of the Confederation. They did take virtually all power over the currency from the states and they did forbid the states, not only to pass bills of attainder, ex post facto laws, and to grant titles of nobility, but also laws impairing the obligation of contracts, a measure copied from the Northwest Ordinance of 1787, a statute always regarded as one of the liberal achievements in our history. In the interests of a uniform currency they gave power to Congress to coin money and regulate its value; they refused to grant to Congress power to issue paper money or to make it legal tender. It is both interesting and significant that there was extremely little opposition to these economic provisions of the Constitution when it was before the state conventions, particularly when one compares the minute amount of opposition to some of these clauses to the great volume of criticism of the new government as being too strongly centralized.

Obviously, localism was the principal basis of Anti-Federalism. The Anti-Federalists were, as a scholar has recently put it, "men of little faith."[30] They distrusted the new system because it would be remote and not so immediately subject to control. They did object to a number of provisions relating to structure, to selection, and to the powers of specific departments, just as they objected to the absence of a bill of rights, but what most of them seemed to want was a continuation of something like the Articles of Confederation, or at least of a much weaker central government than that provided in the proposed Constitution.[31]

If the Framers are not properly characterized as reactionary, it does not follow that they were seventeenth century Levellers, or nineteenth century reformers, nor were they Populists of the 1890's or Progres-

---

[30] Cecelia M. Kenyon, "Men of Little Faith: the Anti-Federalists on the Nature of Representative Government," *William and Mary Quarterly*, Third Series, vol. XII, no. 1, pp. 3-43.

[31] "The last thing in the world they [the Anti-Federalists] wanted was a national democracy which would permit Congressional majorities to operate freely and without restraint." Kenyon, *op. cit.*, p. 43.

sives, whether of the 1912, the 1924, or the 1948 vintage. Nor were they democrats in the sense that Tom Paine and a few, a very few, articulate though minor leaders of sentiment during the Revolution were democrats who wished to have the American constitutions embody the principles accepted two or three generations later: universal male suffrage, freedom for the slaves, together with the view advocated by Paine and others, but not generally accepted in the nineteenth century, simple majority rule rather than separation of powers and checks and balances.

To return to the comparisons suggested at the beginning of the first chapter. Why were the same men in responsible public offices in 1787 as in 1776? Why had the leaders of the Revolution not been ousted, hanged or exiled? Why were the leaders of the Revolution able to keep it to a moderate course, when revolutions as we know of them have usually run through a cycle involving a period of absolutism and frequently a restoration of the old order? And why, finally, were the men of 1776-1787 able to lay the foundations for successful self-government in both the states and the nation?

A full answer to those questions would involve more than has been or could be considered in these chapters. It would include such factors as the absence of feudalism,[32] and the comparatively high degree of economic prosperity in this country. For although there were social and economic cleavages in America, and even enough contemporary awareness of them to speak of class consciousness, there was nothing comparable to the explosive situation which existed in France at the same time. Historians, especially those given to emphasizing economic factors, have made much of Shay's Rebellion as an example of class conflict. But that rebellion was no blindly violent uprising of long-oppressed peasants. It was a comparatively orderly protest of landowners temporarily embarrassed by post-war depression.

Another factor to be considered in explaining the success of the Revolution would be the absence of acute or profound religious conflict. To be sure, there was controversy, and considerable hard feeling in the areas where there had been an established church. But again, this conflict, when compared with the violent struggles between and against churches in other countries, is seen to be in a minor key.

---

[32] Louis Hartz, *The Liberal Tradition in America*, ch. II.

These, and other factors not strictly political in their nature, are relevant. But essential to an understanding of the unique character of the American Revolution is the continuity of its political and constitutional aspects with the experience and institutions of the past. If we read only the Declaration of Independence and some of the speeches, pamphlets and journalistic letters of the fifteen years or so preceding 1776, we get the impression that Parliament or the Crown and Parliament denied Americans the elementary rights of self-government. This is far from the truth. The colonists continued to exercise extraordinary powers of self-government in all colonies, at least until 1774. In some of them, particularly Connecticut and Rhode Island, there was almost complete self-government. It was because the colonists had been virtually self-governing—and continued so—that the financial and administrative measures adopted by Britain after 1760 seemed harsh and reactionary. Edmund Burke understood this clearly when he advised Parliament to "Leave the Americans as they anciently stood. . . ."[33]

This long experience in virtual self-government was essential to the success of independence and of self-government after independence. Because of it, both the people and the leaders whom they selected were politically sophisticated. They were well-read in political theory; they quoted Locke, Montesquieu, Burlamaqui, Grotius, and others with ease. But they were generations ahead of these theorists in the practice of politics. They not only had definite ideas about the ends of government; but they also knew from experience something about the techniques of politics and politicians, and knowing these, they knew something of the difficulties involved in securing the kind of government they wanted.

Perhaps the most important product of this long experience in self-government was consensus. If I seem to belabor this concept, it is because we have so long taken it for granted, and because it has sometimes been obscured by the efforts of historians to trace the outlines of class conflict in this period of our past. But the consensus was there, and it was crucial. Moreover, it was not the consensus of ideology, or desperation, or crisis, or any other that may temporarily unite a people revolting against a specific evil. It was rather the consensus rooted in the common life, habits, institutions, and experience of generations. And furthermore, it was the consensus of contentment and success, not

[33] Speech on American Taxation (1774), *Works* (Bohn ed.) II, p. 432.

misery and oppression. It was therefore durable and flexible, associated with community self-confidence and conducive to moderation.

This consensus, together with long experience in practical politics gave the men of 1776-1787 a capacity for compromise rare in periods of revolutionary upheaval. As I have indicated, there was no necessity for the resolution of issues which were by their nature deeply divisive. On the great principles of liberty and justice, on the general ends and structure of representative government, there was almost universal agreement. As Madison wrote in *The Federalist,* the "genius" of America was republican. Yet on lesser—but not unimportant—questions there was conflict of opinion and interest which might have hardened into irreconcilable disputes. Such, of course, was the question of equal or proportionate representation of the states in the Congress, or the several issues relating to slavery which divided the North and the South. The Constitution, when it was finally signed, was not completely satisfactory to anyone. It embodied no individual's—and no group's—dream of perfection. The fact that both Franklin and Hamilton were willing to sign it reflects not only the degree to which it was a compromise—"a bundle of compromises" if you like—but also the extent of mutual confidence which made compromise possible and acceptable. This willingness to compromise was also a product of the experience of men long accustomed to the untidiness involved in both the procedures and the results of self-government. Our birth as a nation took place when we were already politically mature.

Compromise was not the only aspect of this maturity. Long experience, in local government and in colonial government, had equipped the men of this generation with sheer political "know-how". The leaders of the Revolution were not new to politics. The Revolutionary assemblies were frequently the old colonial legislatures by another name, and minus their Tory membership. Colonial politicians already knew the uses and abuses of republican political techniques. They were, needless to say, skillful propagandists; they knew the dangers of demagogues. They were familiar with the caucus; they were on their guard against "cabals" and intrigues. They were aware of the possibilities of bribery and corruption; they knew something of the role of patronage in building up what we would call a political machine. Knowledge of this sort served as immunization against the kind of disillusionment suffered both by Paine and Hamilton after their initial enthusiasm of

1774-1776. They knew, too, the solid as distinguished from the possibly sordid aspects of political procedure. The easy and efficient use made of committees throughout the entire period is remarkable as a stage in the evolution of representative institutions. It is a technique absolutely essential to this form of government, for it combines the virtue of concentrated attention by a small group with responsibility to the whole. The men of the Revolution, when they used it in the deliberative sphere, used it with practiced skill. They were far less successful, of course, when they used it for executive purposes under the Articles—a fact which they quickly recognized and remedied. This familiarity with and facility in the use of the ordinary procedures of self-government helped to make the transition from colonial to independent status smooth and easy.

Nowhere is their political maturity shown more clearly than in their innovations. Whether in adapting colonial frames of government to the needs of the independent states, or in fashioning a new species of federalism, they achieved much because they did not attempt the impossible. The adage, "politics is the art of the possible," applies as well to the establishment of governments as to the carrying on of governments already established. In state and in nation the Framers worked within the limits set by their inheritance and by the convictions of the people. Had they attempted more, had they sought a transformation of society into something altogether novel and strange to America—a degree of liberty and equality not dreamed of save by a handful of idealists—they might have wrought a miracle. More likely, they would have failed, either immediately or through encouragement of a reaction, compared with which the discontent with the Articles and with economic legislation in the states would seem like placid satisfaction.

Their innovations are more accurately designated inventions. For, in the manner of the great inventors, the Framers worked with what was available and usable; from existing experience and knowledge they devised new institutions which were also improved modifications of those then existing. In doing so they strengthened rather than severed the chain of continuity. These statesmen-inventors were not supermen or demigods. They had human failings—they were not without self-interest—and they did not create, nor did they long for, Utopia. But when we judge them by relevant standards we necessarily conclude that the remarkable degree of their achievement entitles them to a place in the company of the legislators of myth and history who reshaped their country's laws to their country's good.   They followed the ancient example of successful legislators in observing the principle of continuity. They departed from their example in that they worked by and with the consent of the governed.

DATE DUE